Jams&Jellies

Better Homes and Gardens®

Jams & Jellies

OUR
VERY BEST
SWEET &
SAVORY
RECIPES

HOUGHTON MIFFLIN HARCOURT

BOSTON · NEW YORK · 2016

Better Homes and Gardens® Jams & Jellies

Editor: Jan Miller

Project Editor: Shelli McConnell, Purple Pear Publishing, Inc.

Contributing Editor: Ellen Boeke

Contributing Copy Editor and Proofreader: Carrie Truesdell, Terri Fredrickson

Test Kitchen Director: Lynn Blanchard

Test Kitchen Product Supervisor: Colleen Weeden

Test Kitchen Home Economists: Sarah Brekke, Linda Brewer, Carla Christian, Juliana Hale, Sammy Mila, Jill Moberly, Lori Wilson

Contributing Photographers: Karla Conrad, Jason Donnelly, Jacob Fox, Andy Lyons, Blaine Moats

Contributing Stylists: Greg Luna, Sue Mitchell, Dianna Nolin

Administrative Assistants: Barb Allen, Marlene Todd

Special Interest Media

Editorial Leader: Doug Kouma

Editorial Director, Food: Jennifer Dorland Darling

Houghton Mifflin Harcourt

Publisher: Natalie Chapman

Editorial Director: Cindy Kitchel

Executive Editor, Brands: Anne Ficklen

Editorial Associate: Molly Aronica

Managing Editor: Marina Padakis Lowry

Production Director: Tom Hyland

Waterbury Publications, Inc.

Design Director: Ken Carlson

Associate Design Director: Doug Samuelson

Production Assistant: Mindy Samuelson

Our seal assures you that every recipe in *Better Homes and Gardens® Jams & Jellies* has been tested in the Better Homes and Gardens® Test Kitchen. This means that each recipe is practical and reliable and meets our high standards of taste appeal. We guarantee your satisfaction with this book for as long as you own it.

Pictured on front cover:
Clementine Jelly, page 104, Watermelon-Raspberry Jelly, page 148, Classic Strawberry Jam, page 39, Lemon Lime-Orange Marmalade, page 111, Peppery Papaya Jelly, page 119

Pictured on back cover:
Old-Fashioned Grape Jelly, page 25; Nectarine-Blueberry Jam, page 174; Orange & Fennel Marmalade, page 103; Cider 'n' Spice Jelly, page 77

For information about permission to reproduce selections from this book, write to trade.permissions@hmhco.com or to Permissions, Houghton Mifflin Harcourt Publishing Company, 3 Park Avenue, 19th Floor, New York, New York 10016.

www.hmhco.com

Library of Congress Cataloging-in-Publication Data

Title: Better homes and gardens jams & jellies : 110 of our very best sweet & savory recipes.

Other titles: Jams & jellies

Description: Boston : Houghton Mifflin Harcourt, [2016] | Includes index.

Identifiers:
LCCN 2015046884 (print)
LCCN 2016000915 (ebook)
ISBN 9780544715554 (trade paper)
ISBN 9780544715561 (ebook)

Subjects:
LCSH: Jam. | Jelly. | LCGFT: Cookbooks.

Classification:
LCC TX612.J3 B485 2016 (print) |
LCC TX612.J3 (ebook) | DDC

641.85/2—dc23

LC record available at http://lccn.loc.gov/2015046884

Book design by Waterbury Publications, Inc., Des Moines, Iowa.

Printed in the United States of America.

DOW 10 9 8 7 6 5 4 3 2 1

4500586277

Contents

LOOK FOR THESE ICONS:

Beginner These recipes are easy for people who are new to jam and jelly making. With minimal ingredient preparation and straightforward instructions, anyone can find success.

Lower Sugar These recipes use honey in place of sugar or a reduced amount of sugar when compared to the classic version. Lower-sugar pectin is used in many of these recipes.

Jam Session

When gardens and farmers markets are overflowing with fresh produce, it's time to save a little summer in a jar. Gather your canning gear, pick some produce, and schedule a jam session.

Using These **Recipes**

Follow the recipes in this book exactly. They have been tested with ingredients in the correct proportions for success and safety. Remember these tips:

MAKE THE AMOUNT OF JAM SPECIFIED IN THE RECIPE. Do not double the recipe. Doubling can cause problems with jelling and scorching in the pan.

USE THE AMOUNT OF SUGAR SPECIFIED. Don't alter. Sugar interacts with pectin to create the ideal texture. It also acts as a preservative.

ACID IS NEEDED FOR JELLING AND FLAVOR. With low-acid fruits, the recipe will call for lemon juice to achieve a proper pH level (be sure to use bottled lemon juice for best results).

PH PARAMETERS

Essential to proper canning, pH is a scale from 1 to 14 that measures the chemical properties of foods. Foods with a pH of less than 7 are acidic. Foods with a pH of more than 7 are alkaline, or basic. To safely can jams and jellies in a boiling-water canner, they must be acidic. We use a pH meter to ensure the safety of each recipe.

TRUST THE SEAL

Although the threat of foodborne illness in home-preserved foods is real, using a reliable recipe and information source, such as Better Homes and Gardens®, will help you overcome any insecurity when preserving your own food. All the recipes in this book are thoroughly tested in our Test Kitchen for quality, flavor, usability, and safety according to United States Department of Agriculture (USDA) guidelines, and they have earned the Better Homes and Gardens Test Kitchen Seal with guaranteed pH levels. Please follow each recipe exactly to ensure recipe success and safety.

✱ THE POWER OF PECTIN Pectin is a natural substance found in many fruits. It gives jams and jellies thickness and body. Some fruits, such as apples and grapes, contain enough pectin to thicken jams alone; others need a little boost. Pectin comes in powdered and liquid forms and also in a formulation suitable for low-sugar recipes. For best results, use the type of pectin specified in the recipe.

Know Your **Produce**

Choose undamaged and unblemished fruits and vegetables. Small bruises and spots may be trimmed from the food. Use produce within a day or two of harvesting or purchasing.

PEAK OF RIPENESS

Fully ripe yet firm fruit has the best flavor and processes with optimal results. Avoid fruit that is overripe or underripe. Berries and fruits at the peak of their flavor will mash to the correct consistency and produce the most delicious jams and jellies.

PREPPING PRODUCE

First wash the produce. Use only water and rinse thoroughly. (A large colander is helpful.) Peel produce only if the recipe specifies. Some peels are left on because they contain pectin, which helps thicken the product.

EASY PREP TIPS

These techniques will help you prep produce for jams and jellies efficiently and easily.

STRAWBERRIES Remove the stem with a small sharp knife, cutting a cone-shape piece of fruit around the stem. This process is called hulling. A grapefruit spoon also makes short work of hulling.

TOMATOES Make an X at the blossom end of a tomato, then blanch. The X encourages the tomato skin to split so that you can slip it off easily with your fingers after blanching.

APPLES Invest a few dollars in an apple corer to speed up apple coring. Simply push the corer firmly into the apple, twist, and pull.

HOW TO PEEL PEACHES AND TOMATOES

Blanching peaches and tomatoes loosens the skin, making peeling a snap.

1. Bring a large pot of water to boiling. Add peaches or tomatoes, and leave them in 30 to 60 seconds or until skins start to split.

2. Remove and plunge peaches or tomatoes into a large bowl of ice water. Remove them from the cold water when cool enough to handle. Use a knife to easily pull off the skin.

JAMS & JELLIES **TOOLBOX**

Most of what you need for making jams and jellies is already in your kitchen. A few specialty tools—such as a magnetic wand to easily fish lids out of hot water—make the job easier.

KITCHEN ESSENTIALS

HEAVY POT This thick-bottom, straight-sided pot is ideal for cooking jams and jellies without scorching. The recommended size of the pot is indicated in each recipe. If a nonreactive pot is called for, use a stainless-steel or enamel-coated pot.

MEASURING SPOONS Most sets of measuring spoons include 1 tablespoon, 1 teaspoon, ½ teaspoon, and ¼ teaspoon.

MEASURING CUPS Use measuring cups for dry goods, such as sugar. Most come in sets of 1 cup, ½ cup, ⅓ cup, and ¼ cup. Use glass cups for liquids.

HEATPROOF RUBBER SCRAPERS AND WOODEN SPOONS Use these long-handled tools for stirring jams and getting the last bits out of pots.

COLANDER Use to wash and drain produce and to strain juice for jellies and syrups.

FINE-MESH SIEVE Use to rinse small amounts of berries or to remove seeds and skins from pureed fruits.

LADLE A metal ladle is necessary to transfer hot mixtures from one vessel to another. Sterilize ladles by dipping them into boiling water.

RULER Use a ruler to measure headspace when filling jars.

TONGS If you do not have a magnetic wand, use long-handled tongs to remove lids, screw bands, and jars from boiling water.

100-PERCENT-COTTON CHEESECLOTH Use cheesecloth to line a colander or sieve to strain juice from fruits. Cheesecloth can be gathered around fruit and squeezed to remove juice.

KITCHEN TOWELS These have many uses when canning. Use one to wipe rims of jars. Lay a dry towel on the counter to set hot jars on (never set hot jars directly on the counter; they may crack). Lint-free towels are the best.

POT HOLDERS One pair is essential, but two are better so you will always have a clean, dry pair. Do not use wet or sticky pot holders.

TIMER A timer is important to keep track of cooking and processing times.

PERMANENT MARKER OR DECORATIVE LABELS Use the marker to write contents and dates on lids. Add decorative labels to jars that will be given as gifts (see Sweet Gifts, page 228).

CANNING ESSENTIALS

BOILING-WATER CANNER This is simply a large pot with a rack in the bottom and a lid on top. The rack allows water to flow beneath the jars for even heating. The rack also has handles that allow you to lift and lower the jars into the boiling water. The contents of the jars are heated to a temperature of 212°F, which is hot enough to kill bacteria.

JAR FUNNEL Wider and shorter than other funnels, jar funnels are invaluable for preventing spills when quickly filling jars. Sterilize in boiling water with the jars.

MAGNETIC WAND This magic wand is used to drop lids into the hot water to soften the sealing compound and then easily lift the lids from the hot water.

JAR LIFTER This tool lifts jars securely in and out of hot water. Use two hands if possible, and squeeze firmly.

 CREATE A CANNER You don't have to buy a boiling-water canner to make jams and jellies. You can use a large pot that has a well-fitting lid and is deep enough so that jars are covered with 1 to 2 inches of water. However, you will need a rack to set jars up off the bottom to allow water to flow under them. Make your own rack by wiring together lid rings to fit into the pot.

JAR BASICS

The type of jars you use for canning is just as important as how you get them ready for use. Canning jars are molded from thick glass designed to withstand processing year after year. Most jam and jelly recipes call for half-pint jars, and you may choose between regular- and wide-mouth. Recipes will specify jar sizes.

8-OUNCE JELLY JARS (half pint) These jars have straight sides and sometimes an imprinted pattern on the outsides.

4-OUNCE JARS These smaller jars are perfect for gift-giving or if you want to open a small amount at a time. Process the same amount of time as for half-pint jars.

PLASTIC FREEZER JARS The thick plastic of these jars makes them ideal for freezer jams because there is no danger of cracking in the freezer.

SCREW BANDS Metal bands secure lids to the jars during processing and can be removed before storage. Bands can be reused. Be sure bands are free of rust and dents, and wash in hot, soapy water before and after each use.

LIDS These flat round pieces are for one-time use. When purchasing new jars, lids and bands will be included, but you can purchase additional lids separately. The red substance on the underside of the lid helps seal the lid onto the jar, ensuring an airtight seal.

STERILIZING JARS

All jars must be cleaned and sterilized before using. Wash empty jars in hot, soapy water; rinse well. Place jars in the boiling-water canner or a separate large pot. Cover jars with hot water (jars must be submerged). Bring to boiling; reduce heat. Sterilize jars by boiling gently for 10 minutes. Keep jars in simmering water until needed. (If using a separate pot for sterilizing, fill canner half-full with water; bring to boiling. Use hot water from the sterilizing pot to top off water in canner after jars are added.)

Remove one jar at a time for filling. Use a jar lifter or tongs to grasp jar and carefully pour water out into pot. Fill jar as directed (page 16) and return to boiling-water canner to keep hot. Take another jar from the hot water and fill it: One jar out, one jar in (this maintains sterile conditions rather than filling assembly-line style). Process as directed (page 16).

NOTE: Don't boil lids to sterilize them. This can prevent proper sealing. Place lids in a bowl and ladle some boiling water from the sterilizing pot over them to soften the red sealing compound.

QUESTIONS & **ANSWERS**

If you're new to the canning game, you'll probably have a question or two as you proceed.
Here are some questions frequently asked.

Q Can I process a jar that is only partially full?

A No. If you have remaining mixture that won't fill a jar to the recommended headspace, cover and refrigerate the leftovers. Partially full jars may not seal correctly and are not considered safe.

Q Do I have to squeeze fresh lemons when a recipe calls for lemon juice?

A No. Unless the recipe specifies freshly squeezed juice, it is better to use bottled lemon juice for canning. The pH level of bottled lemon juice is consistent; the pH level in fresh lemons may vary.

Q Rather than sterilizing my canning jars in boiling water, can I use my dishwasher to sterilize them?

A Even though some dishwashers provide a high-heat sanitizing cycle, the temperature reached in that cycle is only about 160°F, which is 52°F below the temperature of boiling water. For that reason, the only safe way to sterilize canning jars is in boiling water (*opposite*).

Q My grandmother covered her hot jams and jellies with a thick layer of melted wax or paraffin instead of using a boiling-water canner. Why can't I do this too?

A Your grandmother's method was popular for decades, but it is no longer considered safe. Paraffin does not form an airtight seal and is easily dislocated when jars are moved. It is also prone to mold and other bacterial growth.

KNOW YOUR **SPREADS**

This book contains recipes for making and canning so much more than jams and jellies.
Discover the subtle but distinct differences that define fruit and vegetable spreads.

JAMS are made by cooking crushed or chopped fruit with sugar until thick and spreadable. Although chunks of fruit are desirable, jams are less firm than jellies.

JELLIES are made from fruit juice, sugar, and pectin (either naturally occurring in fruit or packaged). Jellies can be made with purchased juice or juice extracted from fresh fruit.

PRESERVES consist of chunks of fruit in a soft jelly. The fruit pieces are larger and retain more texture than those in jams. Marmalades fall into this category.

CHUTNEY is a flavorful mixture of fruit, vinegar, sugar, and spices. Its texture ranges from chunky to fine.

COMPOTES are made in the same process as syrup, except syrup is the base in which small chunks of fruit are suspended.

CONSERVE takes jam a step further with the addition of chunky fruit or dried fruit and/or nuts.

FRUIT BUTTER is an extra-sweet blend of fruit and spices that simmers down to a spreadably smooth, butterlike consistency.

SYRUPS are made by cooking fruit, extracting the juice, and cooking the juice with sugar until it is a thick consistency.

CANNING **JAMS & JELLIES**

Processing jams and jellies in a boiling-water canner heats the food to kill bacteria and is also the first step in creating a sealed jar. Follow these steps for making jams and jellies that can safely be stored at room temperature in your pantry.

1 Unless otherwise specified in the recipe, bring mixture to a full rolling boil. (Bubbles break the surface so rapidly you can't stir them down.)

2 Boiling makes foam. To skim off foam, gently glide a metal spoon over the surface; remove and discard the frothy bubbles. A wide, shallow spoon works best.

3 Use a canning funnel and ladle for filling jars. A funnel helps prevent sticky liquid from running down the outside of the jar.

4 When filling jars, leave the recommended headspace (the space between the top of the mixture and the rim). Headspace gives room for food to expand when heated and allows a vacuum seal to form. Measure on the outside of the jar.

5 Use a clean, damp cloth to wipe jar rims. Food particles or liquid left on the jar rim might interfere with the seal. If the jar is too hot to touch, hold it with a dry towel or pot holder.

6 Use a magnetic wand or tongs to transfer a lid from hot water to jar. Do not touch the underside of the lid.

7 Add a band, adjusting it no more than fingertip tight—just tight enough that you could turn the band another ¼ to ½ inch tighter. If applied too tightly, the lid might not seal.

8 As you fill each jar, one at a time, set it into the canner filled with simmering water. The canner shown (opposite) has a rack with handles that hang on the canner rim so it is easier to load. In this case, after each jar is added to the rack, lower the rack back into the water to keep jars hot while you finish with the remaining jars. If you don't have a rack, use a jar lifter to lower each jar into the water as it is filled. When all jars are filled and the rack is lowered into the canner, if necessary add additional hot water to the canner until the jars are covered with 1 to 2 inches of water. Cover; heat to a full rolling boil. Start processing time from the moment the water starts to boil. Keep at a low, rolling boil.

9 When processing time is up, turn off heat. Using pot holders, lift up the rack and rest handles on the side of the canner. Use a jar lifter to transfer jars to a wire rack or onto a kitchen towel. Leave at least 1 inch of space between jars to allow air to circulate. Do not tighten bands. Let jars set undisturbed for 12 to 24 hours. (Do not turn jars over while cooling to try to redistribute the fruit; it could break the set.) Check to see if the jars have sealed (opposite). If desired, remove screw bands. Wipe the jar rims, if necessary. Label jars with contents and date. Store in a cool, dry, dark place for up to 1 year.

IS IT SEALED?

A vacuum seal is needed for long-term storage of jams and jellies. Each canning lid has a raised circle in the center. After canning, if a vacuum seal has been created, that raised circle is sucked down tight (while the jars are cooling, you will hear a loud pop from each jar as the vacuum is formed). Test the seal by firmly pressing your finger on the center of the lid. It should not give. If it makes a popping sound, it is not properly sealed. If a jar fails to seal, refrigerate it immediately and use the contents within 3 weeks.

★ TEST KITCHEN TIP If using a smaller jar than called for in the recipe, process for the same length of time. If using a pint jar, add 5 minutes to the processing time to ensure the contents are getting heated through.

Turn your favorite bottle of juice into a spread for your bread. The prep is easy with no cutting, mashing, or straining required.

Juice Jelly

3 cups bottled unsweetened grape juice; purple carrot, beet, and green apple vegetable juice blend with fruit; yellow and orange carrot, sweet potato, and orange vegetable juice blend with fruit; apple juice or apple cider; orange juice; or cranberry juice

1 1.75-oz. pkg. regular powdered fruit pectin or 6 Tbsp. classic powdered fruit pectin

4½ cups sugar

1. In a 6- to 8-quart heavy pot combine juice and pectin. Bring to a full rolling boil, stirring constantly. Stir in sugar. Return to a full rolling boil, stirring constantly. Boil hard 1 minute, stirring constantly. Remove pot from heat. Quickly skim off foam with a metal spoon.

2. Ladle hot jelly into hot, sterilized half-pint canning jars, leaving a ¼-inch headspace. Wipe jar rims; adjust lids and screw bands.

3. Process filled jars in a boiling-water canner 5 minutes (start timing when water returns to boiling). Remove jars form canner; cool on wire racks. **Makes 5 half-pint jars.**

PER 1 TABLESPOON: 57 cal., 0 g fat, 0 mg chol., 2 mg sodium, 14 g carb., 14 g sugars, 0 g fiber, 0 g pro.

PREP: 35 MINUTES   **STAND:** 24 HOURS

With one easy formula, fill your freezer with picked-fresh flavor. Freezer jam is a great alternative to canning with no special equipment needed.

Strawberry Freezer Jam

4   cups hulled fresh strawberries

4   cups sugar

½   tsp. lemon zest

1   1.75-oz. pkg. regular powdered fruit pectin or
    6 Tbsp. classic powdered fruit pectin

¾   cup water

1. In a large bowl use a potato masher to crush the berries until you have 2 cups. Mix berries, sugar, and lemon zest. Let stand 10 minutes, stirring occasionally. In a small saucepan combine pectin and the water. Bring to boiling; boil 1 minute, stirring constantly. Add to berry mixture; stir about 3 minutes or until sugar is dissolved and mixture is no longer grainy.

2. Ladle jam into half-pint freezer containers, leaving a ½-inch headspace. Seal and label. Let stand at room temperature 24 hours or until set. Store up to 3 weeks in the refrigerator or up to 1 year in the freezer. **Makes 5 half-pint jars.**

PER 1 TABLESPOON: 41 cal., 0 g fat, 0 mg chol., 0 mg sodium, 11 g carb., 10 g sugars, 0 g fiber, 0 g pro.

SPICED PEACH Substitute 3 cups finely chopped, peeled peaches for strawberries. Omit zest. Add 2 Tbsp. lemon juice. Increase sugar to 4½ cups and stir in ½ tsp. apple pie spice with sugar.

RASPBERRY-ORANGE Substitute 6 cups fresh raspberries for the strawberries; mash and measure 3 cups. Increase sugar to 5¼ cups. Substitute orange zest for lemon zest.

BLACKBERRY-LIME Substitute 6 cups fresh blackberries for the strawberries; mash and measure 3 cups. Increase sugar to 5¼ cups. Substitute lime zest for lemon zest.

BLUEBERRY-CINNAMON Substitute 5 cups fresh blueberries for the strawberries; mash and measure 3 cups. Increase sugar to 5¼ cups. Stir in 1 teaspoon ground cinnamon with the sugar.

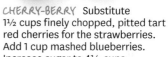

MANGO-PINEAPPLE Substitute 4 mangoes, seeded, peeled, and cubed, for the strawberries. Mash the mangoes and measure 3 cups. Omit lemon zest and use ¼ cup pineapple juice. Increase sugar to 5 cups.

CHERRY-BERRY Substitute 1½ cups finely chopped, pitted tart red cherries for the strawberries. Add 1 cup mashed blueberries. Increase sugar to 4½ cups.

APRICOT-TANGERINE Substitute 2½ cups finely chopped fresh apricots for the strawberries. Omit lemon zest and add 2 Tbsp. tangerine or orange juice. Increase sugar to 5½ cups.

STRAWBERRY-RHUBARB Decrease strawberries to 1½ cups mashed and add 1 cup finely chopped fresh rhubarb. Increase sugar to 5 cups.

PEAR-RASPBERRY Substitute 3 cups finely chopped, peeled fresh pears for the strawberries. Add 1 cup crushed raspberries. Increase sugar to 5 cups and add ¼ tsp. anise flavoring.

CHAPTER 1

Beautiful Berries

Old-Fashioned Grape Jelly

6 lb. Concord grapes
(use about 4½ lb. fully
ripe grapes plus about
1½ lb. firm, slightly less
ripe grapes)

¾ cup water

3¾ cups sugar

1. Wash and stem grapes. In a 6- to 8-quart heavy pot crush grapes with a potato masher. Add the water. Bring to boiling; reduce heat. Simmer, covered, about 10 minutes or until grapes are very soft.

2. Line a colander with several layers of 100-percent-cotton cheesecloth. Place colander over a large bowl. Pour grapes and cooking liquid into colander. Let stand at room temperature 4½ hours. Measure about 7 cups grape juice. Discard seeds and cooked skins in colander. Cover and chill the juice 12 to 14 hours.

3. Using clean cheesecloth, line colander with several layers of 100-percent-cotton cheesecloth; set colander over a large bowl. Strain chilled juice through cheesecloth, straining out sediment; discard cheesecloth.

4. Place strained juice in the same pot. Add sugar. Bring to a full rolling boil, stirring to dissolve sugar. Boil hard, uncovered, about 20 minutes or until jelly sheets off a metal spoon and reaches 220°F (see page 78). Remove from heat. Skim off foam with a metal spoon.

5. Ladle hot jelly into hot, sterilized half-pint canning jars, leaving a ¼-inch headspace. Wipe jar rims; adjust lids and screw bands.

6. Process filled jars in a boiling-water canner 5 minutes (start timing when water returns to boiling). Remove jars from canner; cool on wire racks. **Makes 5 half-pint jars.**

PER 1 TABLESPOON: 69 cal., 0 g fat, 0 mg chol., 1 mg sodium, 18 g carb., 17 g sugars, 0 g fiber, 0 g pro.

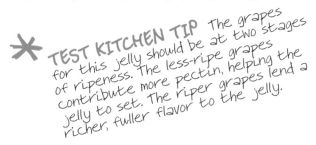

★ TEST KITCHEN TIP The grapes for this jelly should be at two stages of ripeness. The less-ripe grapes contribute more pectin, helping the jelly to set. The riper grapes lend a richer, fuller flavor to the jelly.

Grape Jam

3   to 3½ lb. Concord grapes

2   cups water

4½   cups sugar

1. Wash and stem grapes. Measure 8 cups. Remove skins from half of the grapes by gently squeezing until pulp pops out of stem ends. Set grapes aside.

2. In an 8- to 10-quart heavy pot combine the skinned and unskinned grapes. Cover and cook 10 minutes or until very soft. Press grapes through a sieve or food mill; discard seeds and cooked skins. Measure 3 cups of strained pulp; return to pot. Stir in the uncooked grape skins and the water. Cook, covered, 10 minutes. Uncover; stir in sugar. Bring mixture to a full rolling boil, stirring often. Boil, uncovered, 18 to 24 minutes or until jam sheets off a metal spoon (see page 78). Remove pot from heat. Quickly skim off foam with a metal spoon.

3. Ladle hot jam into hot, sterilized half-pint canning jars, leaving a ¼-inch headspace. Wipe jar rims; adjust lids and screw bands.

4. Process filled jars in a boiling-water canner 10 minutes (start timing when water returns to boiling). Remove jars from canner; cool on wire racks until set. **Makes 6 half-pint jars.**

PER 1 TABLESPOON: 42 cal., 0 g fat, 0 mg chol., 0 mg sodium, 11 g carb., 11 g sugars, 0 g fiber, 0 g pro.

✳ TEST KITCHEN TIP Concord grapes are often quite seedy. A food mill makes short work of separating the seeds from the pulp. If you have one of these handy tools, use it for jam making.

PREP: 40 MINUTES PROCESS: 10 MINUTES

strawberries should be unblemished, deeply colored, slightly soft, and quite fragrant. Choose small berries if you can; they boast the biggest flavor.

Classic Strawberry Jam

12 cups fresh strawberries, hulled

1 1.75-oz. pkg. regular powdered fruit pectin or 6 Tbsp. classic powdered fruit pectin

½ tsp. butter

7 cups sugar

1. Place 1 cup of the strawberries in an 8-quart heavy pot. Use a potato masher to crush berries. Continue adding strawberries and crushing until you have 5 cups crushed berries.

2. Stir pectin and butter into crushed strawberries in pot. Bring to a full rolling boil, stirring constantly. Stir in sugar. Return to a full rolling boil, stirring constantly. Boil hard 1 minute, stirring constantly. Remove from heat. Quickly skim off foam with a metal spoon.

3. Ladle hot jam into hot, sterilized half-pint canning jars, leaving a ¼-inch headspace. Wipe jar rims; adjust lids and screw bands.

4. Process filled jars in a boiling-water canner 10 minutes (start timing when water returns to boiling). Remove jars from canner; cool on wire racks.* **Makes 10 half-pint jars.**

*NOTE: The jam may need to stand 1 to 2 weeks after canning to become fully set.

STRAWBERRY-BALSAMIC PINK PEPPERCORN JAM: Prepare as directed, except stir in ½ cup balsamic vinegar with the pectin and butter. Stir in ¼ cup pink peppercorns after skimming off foam. Stir jam before serving.

STRAWBERRY-GINGER ALE JAM: Prepare as directed, except stir in ½ cup ginger ale or strawberry-flavor carbonated beverage after skimming off foam.

STRAWBERRY-MARSALA-THYME JAM: Prepare as directed, except stir in ½ cup Marsala wine with the pectin and butter. Stir in ¼ cup snipped fresh thyme after skimming off foam.

PER 1 TABLESPOON CLASSIC, STRAWBERRY-BALSAMIC, STRAWBERRY-GINGER ALE, OR STRAWBERRY-MARSALA-THYME VARIATIONS: 39 cal., 0 g fat, 0 mg chol., 1 mg sodium, 10 g carb., 9 g sugars, 0 g fiber, 0 g pro.

STRAWBERRY-KUMQUAT JAM: In a small heavy saucepan combine 1 cup quartered kumquats (large seeds removed) and 1 cup water. Bring to boiling; reduce heat. Simmer, covered, about 20 minutes or until kumquats are tender; drain. Prepare jam as directed, except reduce crushed strawberries to 4 cups and add kumquats after crushing berries. **Makes about 8 half-pint jars.**

PER 1 TABLESPOON: 48 cal., 0 g fat, 0 mg chol., 1 mg sodium, 12 g carb., 9 g sugars, 0 g fiber, 0 g pro.

Strawberry-Cranberry Jam

3 lb. fresh strawberries, hulled

¾ cup dried cranberries

1 1.75-oz. pkg. regular powdered fruit pectin or 6 Tbsp. classic powdered fruit pectin

7 cups sugar

1 tsp. butter

1. Place 1 cup of the strawberries in an 8-quart heavy pot. Use a potato masher to crush berries. Continue adding strawberries and crushing until you have 5 cups crushed berries.

2. Stir cranberries and pectin into crushed strawberries in pot. Bring to a full rolling boil, stirring constantly. Add sugar and butter all at once. Return to a full rolling boil; boil hard 1 minute, stirring constantly. Remove from heat; quickly skim off foam with a metal spoon.

3. Ladle hot jam into hot, sterilized half-pint canning jars, leaving a ¼-inch headspace. Wipe jar rims; adjust lids.

4. Process filled jars in a boiling-water canner 10 minutes (start timing when water returns to boiling). Remove jars from canner; cool on wire racks. **Makes 9 half-pint jars.**

PER 1 TABLESPOON: 52 cal., 0 g fat, 0 mg chol., 0 mg sodium, 13 g carb., 13 g sugars, 0 g fiber, 0 g pro.

✳ **TEST KITCHEN TIP** During processing, the fruit pieces may float to the surface of the jam. If this happens, do not tilt, shake, or cool jars upside down to distribute the fruit more evenly. Instead, stir the jam before serving to evenly distribute the fruit.

Strawberry-Lemon Marmalade

2   medium lemons

½   cup water

⅛   tsp. baking soda

3   cups crushed, hulled fresh strawberries (about 6 cups whole berries)

5   cups sugar

½   of a 6-oz. pkg. (1 foil pouch) liquid fruit pectin

1. Score the peel of each lemon into four lengthwise sections; remove the peels with your fingers. Use a sharp knife to scrape off the white portions of peels; discard. Cut peels into thin strips.

2. In a large saucepan combine lemon peel strips, the water, and baking soda. Bring to a boil; reduce heat. Simmer, covered, 20 minutes. Do not drain. Section lemons, reserving juice; discard seeds. Add lemon sections and juice to peel mixture in saucepan. Stir in crushed strawberries. Return to boiling; reduce heat. Simmer, covered, 10 minutes.

3. In an 8- to 10-quart heavy pot combine lemon-strawberry mixture and sugar. Bring to a full rolling boil, stirring constantly. Quickly stir in pectin. Return to a full rolling boil, stirring constantly. Boil hard 1 minute, stirring constantly. Remove from heat. Quickly skim off foam with a metal spoon.

4. Ladle hot marmalade into hot, sterilized half-pint canning jars, leaving a ¼-inch headspace. Wipe jar rims; adjust lids and screw bands.

5. Process filled jars in a boiling-water canner 5 minutes (start timing when water returns to boiling). Remove jars from canner; cool on wire racks. Let stand at room temperature 2 weeks before serving. **Makes 6 half-pint jars.**

PER 1 TABLESPOON: 44 cal., 0 g fat, 0 mg chol., 2 mg sodium, 11 g carb., 11 g sugars, 0 g fiber, 0 g pro.

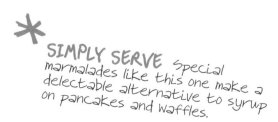

* SIMPLY SERVE special marmalades like this one make a delectable alternative to syrup on pancakes and waffles.

Blueberry-Strawberry Jam

4¾ cups fresh blueberries

4¾ cups fresh strawberries, hulled

1 cup water

3 Tbsp. bottled lemon juice

½ tsp. ground cinnamon

4½ Tbsp. powdered fruit pectin for low- or no-sugar recipes

1. In an 8- to 10-quart pot crush 1 cup of the blueberries with a potato masher. Continue adding blueberries and strawberries and crushing until you have 6 cups crushed berries. Stir in the water, lemon juice, and cinnamon. Gradually stir in pectin. Bring to a full rolling boil, stirring constantly. Boil hard 1 minute, stirring constantly. Remove from heat. Quickly skim off foam with a metal spoon.

2. Ladle hot jam into hot, sterilized half-pint jars, leaving a ¼-inch headspace. Wipe jar rims; adjust lids and screw bands.

3. Process filled jars in a boiling-water canner 10 minutes (start timing when water returns to boiling). Remove jars from canner; cool on wire racks. **Makes 6 half-pint jars.**

PER 1 TABLESPOON: 7 cal., 0 g fat, 0 mg chol., 0 mg sodium, 2 g carb., 1 g sugars, 0 g fiber, 0 g pro.

* TEST KITCHEN TIP Because sugar affects how pectin works and this recipe does not contain sugar, use pectin made specifically for lower-sugar recipes.

Blackberry-Lime Compote

2 limes

4 cups fresh blackberries

3 cups sugar

¼ cup water

1. Remove 1 tablespoon zest and squeeze ½ cup juice from limes. In a 6-quart nonreactive heavy pot combine lime zest, lime juice, and the remaining ingredients. Bring to boiling, stirring until sugar dissolves; reduce heat. Simmer, uncovered, about 25 minutes or until mixture is thickened and reduced to 3 cups, stirring occasionally.

2. Ladle hot compote into hot, sterilized half-pint canning jars, leaving a ¼-inch headspace. Wipe jar rims; adjust lids and screw bands.

3. Process filled jars in a boiling-water canner 15 minutes (start timing when water returns to boiling). Remove jars from canner; cool on wire racks. **Makes 3 half-pint jars.**

PER ¼ CUP: 218 cal., 0 g fat, 0 mg chol., 1 mg sodium, 56 g carb., 53 g sugars, 3 g fiber, 1 g pro.

* SIMPLY SERVE Keep the home-canning theme going by making panna cotta or cheesecake in jelly jars and topping each serving with this tangy compote.

Honey & Thyme Blackberry Jam

9½ to 10 cups fresh blackberries (3¼ to 3½ lb.)

1 1.75-oz. pkg. powdered fruit pectin for lower-sugar recipes or 3 Tbsp. powdered fruit pectin for low- or no-sugar recipes

¼ cup sugar

2 cups honey

2 Tbsp. snipped fresh thyme

1. In a 4- to 6-quart heavy pot crush 1 cup of the blackberries with a potato masher. Continue adding berries and crushing until you have 6 cups crushed berries. Stir in pectin and sugar. Bring to a full rolling boil, stirring constantly. Stir in honey. Return to a full rolling boil, stirring constantly. Boil hard 1 minute, stirring constantly. Remove from heat. Quickly skim off foam with a metal spoon. Stir in thyme.

2. Ladle hot jam into hot, sterilized half-pint canning jars, leaving a ¼-inch headspace. Wipe jar rims; adjust lids and screw bands.

3. Process filled jars in a boiling-water canner 10 minutes (start timing when water returns to boiling). Remove jars from canner; cool on wire racks. **Makes 8 half-pint jars.**

PER 1 TABLESPOON: 22 cal., 0 g fat, 0 mg chol., 0 mg sodium, 6 g carb., 5 g sugars, 1 g fiber, 0 g pro.

* SIMPLY SERVE During summer grilling season, dress up grilled pork and lamb chops with this sweet-savory jam. In the winter, bring sweet memories of summer to the table by serving it with roasted meats.

Cracked black pepper adds a surprise kick to this honey-sweetened jam. Adding only a little pepper makes a big impression.

Honey-Berry Freezer Jam

3 cups hulled, quartered fresh strawberries (1 lb.)

1 cup fresh blackberries

1 large Granny Smith or other tart apple, peeled, cored, and shredded (1 cup)

1 cup honey

1 Tbsp. lemon juice

¼ tsp. cracked black pepper

1. In a medium saucepan combine the first four ingredients (through honey). Bring to boiling over medium-high heat; reduce heat. Simmer, uncovered, about 20 minutes or until slightly thickened (mixture will thicken more as it cools). Stir mixture occasionally while cooking, using a wooden spoon to gently crush the blackberries against the side of the saucepan.

2. Stir in lemon juice and pepper. Remove from heat; cool about 2 hours or until room temperature.

3. Ladle jam into clean half-pint freezer containers, leaving a ½-inch headspace. Seal and label. Let stand at room temperature 24 hours before storing.

4. Store in the freezer up to 1 year or in the refrigerator up to 3 weeks. **Makes 3 half-pint containers.**

PER 1 TABLESPOON: 28 cal., 0 g fat, 0 mg chol., 0 mg sodium, 7 g carb., 7 g sugars, 0 g fiber, 0 g pro.

Raspberry Jam

12 cups fresh raspberries

1 1.75-oz. pkg. regular powdered fruit pectin or 6 Tbsp. powdered fruit pectin

½ tsp. butter

7 cups sugar

1. Place 1 cup of the raspberries in an 8-quart heavy pot. Use a potato masher to crush berries. Continue adding raspberries and crushing until you have 5 cups crushed berries.

2. Stir in pectin and butter. Bring to a full rolling boil, stirring constantly. Stir sugar. Return to full rolling boil, stirring constantly. Boil hard 1 minute, stirring constantly. Remove from heat; quickly skim off foam with a metal spoon.

3. Ladle hot jam into hot, sterilized half-pint canning jars, leaving a ¼-inch headspace. Wipe jar rims; adjust lids and screw bands.

4. Process filled jars in a boiling-water canner 10 minutes (start timing when water returns to boiling). Remove jars from canner; cool on wire racks. **Makes 8 half-pint jars.**

PER 1 TABLESPOON: 59 cal., 0 g fat, 0 mg chol., 0 mg sodium, 15 g carb., 14 g sugars, 1 g fiber, 0 g pro.

✻ TEST KITCHEN TIP If you like, add one of the following to the fruit mixture along with the sugar: 1 teaspoon lemon zest, ½ teaspoon freshly grated nutmeg, or ¼ teaspoon grated fresh ginger. Add a little breakfast to a toasted ham and cheese sandwich by spreading it with one of these tasty flavor options.

Chia seeds are packed with fiber and omega-3 fatty acids. Once they are soaked in liquid, the seeds form a gel that works to set this jam without added pectin.

Very Berry Chia Seed Jam

2 cups sliced, hulled fresh strawberries

2 cups fresh blueberries

2 cups fresh raspberries

½ cup honey

6 inches stick cinnamon (2 sticks)

⅓ cup chia seeds

1. In a large heavy saucepan combine half of the berries and the honey. Bring just to boiling, stirring frequently; reduce heat to medium low. Simmer, uncovered, 5 minutes. Remove saucepan from heat.

2. Lightly mash berry mixture with a potato masher or fork. Stir in the remaining berries, the stick cinnamon, and chia seeds. Bring just to boiling; reduce heat. Simmer, uncovered, about 10 minutes or until thickened. Remove from heat. Remove and discard cinnamon sticks.

3. Ladle jam into clean half-pint freezer containers, leaving a ¼-inch headspace. Seal and label. Store in the refrigerator up to 3 weeks or in the freezer up to 1 year. **Makes 2 half-pint containers.**

PER 1 TABLESPOON: 38 cal., 1 g fat (0 g sat. fat), 0 mg chol., 1 mg sodium, 8 g carb., 6 g sugars, 2 g fiber, 1 g pro.

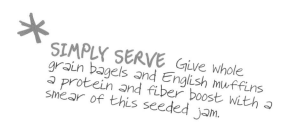

* SIMPLY SERVE Give whole grain bagels and English muffins a protein and fiber boost with a smear of this seeded jam.

Gem Stones

Sweet Cherry Jam

2 lemons

4 cups chopped, pitted fully ripe dark sweet cherries (3 lb.)

1 1.75-oz. pkg. regular powdered fruit pectin or 6 Tbsp. classic powdered fruit pectin

5 cups sugar

1. Remove 1 teaspoon zest and squeeze ¼ cup juice from lemons.

2. In a 6- to 8-quart heavy pot combine cherries, lemon zest, lemon juice, and pectin. Bring to a full rolling boil, stirring constantly. Stir in sugar. Return to a full rolling boil, stirring constantly. Boil hard 1 minute, stirring constantly. Remove from heat. Quickly skim off foam with a metal spoon.

3. Ladle hot jam into hot, sterilized half-pint canning jars, leaving a ¼-inch headspace. Wipe jar rims; adjust lids and screw bands.

4. Process filled jars in a boiling-water canner 10 minutes (start timing when water returns to boiling). Remove jars from canner; cool on wire racks. **Makes 6 half-pint jars.**

PER 1 TABLESPOON: 60 cal., 0 g fat, 0 mg chol., 0 mg sodium, 15 g carb., 15 g sugars, 0 g fiber, 0 g pro.

* TEST KITCHEN TIP A cherry pitter, available from cookware shops, makes removing pits from cherries easy. Pitters work best, but in a pinch, use a clean paper clip. Insert the clip into the stem end of the cherry, twist it around, and pop out the pit.

Dark-roast coffee beans steep in steaming cherry juice to contribute subtle coffee undertones. Make sure to use the freshest beans and darkest roast you can find.

Tart Cherry-Coffee Preserves

½ cup unsweetened cherry juice

⅓ cup whole Italian-roast coffee beans

6¼ cups sugar

5 cups fresh tart red cherries, pitted and coarsely chopped, or 5 cups frozen pitted tart red cherries, coarsely chopped

1 6-oz. pkg. (2 foil pouches) liquid fruit pectin

1. In a small saucepan bring cherry juice to boiling. Stir in coffee beans; cover and remove from heat. Let stand 30 minutes. Strain mixture through a fine-mesh sieve, reserving juice. Discard coffee beans.

2. In a 6- to 8-quart heavy pot combine the reserved cherry juice, the sugar, and cherries. Bring to a full rolling boil, stirring constantly. Quickly stir in pectin. Return to a full rolling boil, stirring constantly. Boil hard 1 minute, stirring constantly. Remove from heat. Quickly skim off foam with a metal spoon.

3. Ladle hot preserves into hot, sterilized half-pint canning jars, leaving a ¼-inch headspace. Wipe jar rims; adjust lids and screw bands.

4. Process filled jars in a boiling-water canner 10 minutes (start timing when water returns to boiling). Remove jars from canner; cool on wire racks. **Makes 6 half-pint jars.**

PER 1 TABLESPOON: 51 cal., 0 g fat, 0 mg chol., 1 mg sodium, 13 g carb., 13 g sugars, 0 g fiber, 0 g pro.

* TEST KITCHEN TIP To get the same results using either fresh or frozen cherries, make sure to measure the fresh cherries before you pit them. The frozen cherries are already pitted, so measure them when they are still frozen.

Tart Cherry Jelly

2 lb. fresh tart red cherries or two 16-oz. pkg. frozen pitted tart red cherries

1 1.75-oz. pkg. regular powdered fruit pectin or 6 Tbsp. classic powdered fruit pectin

4½ cups sugar

1. Place unpitted fresh cherries or frozen cherries in a 6- to 8-quart heavy pot. Add 2 cups water. Bring to simmering (do not boil). Simmer, uncovered, about 15 minutes or until soft and the skins of the cherries start to split. Using a potato masher, carefully crush cherries. Remove from heat.

2. Place a fine-mesh sieve over a large bowl. Ladle cherries into sieve. Using the back of a large spoon, press cherries to release juice; discard pits and pulp. Line a colander with a double layer of 100-percent-cotton cheesecloth; place over a large bowl. Strain juice through cheesecloth; do not squeeze cheesecloth or jelly may be cloudy. Measure 3½ cups juice. Discard pulp in cheesecloth.

3. In the same pot stir together the 3½ cups cherry juice and the pectin. Bring to a full rolling boil, stirring constantly. Add sugar. Return to a full rolling boil, stirring constantly. Boil hard 1 minute, stirring constantly. Remove from heat. Quickly skim off foam with a metal spoon.

4. Ladle hot jelly into hot, sterilized half-pint canning jars, leaving a ¼-inch headspace. Wipe rims; adjust lids and screw bands.

5. Process filled jars in a boiling-water canner 5 minutes (start timing when water returns to boiling). Remove jars from canner; cool on wire racks. **Makes 6 half-pint jars.**

PER 1 TABLESPOON: 51 cal., 0 g fat, 0 mg chol., 0 mg sodium, 13 g carb., 12 g sugars, 0 g fiber, 0 g pro.

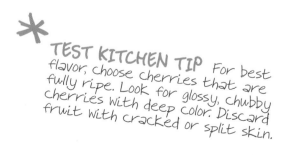

* TEST KITCHEN TIP For best flavor, choose cherries that are fully ripe. Look for glossy, chubby cherries with deep color. Discard fruit with cracked or split skin.

Apricot-Rosemary Jelly

3 lb. fresh apricots, pitted and coarsely chopped (about 9 cups)

3 cups water

5 3-inch sprigs fresh rosemary

1 1.75-oz. pkg. regular powdered fruit pectin or 6 Tbsp. classic powdered fruit pectin

4½ cups sugar

1. In a large pot combine chopped apricots, the water, and rosemary sprigs. Bring to boiling; reduce heat. Simmer, covered, about 20 minutes or until apricots are soft.

2. Line a colander with several layers of 100-percent-cotton cheesecloth. Place colander over a large bowl. Spoon apricot mixture into colander. Let stand 5 to 10 minutes or until juice is drained. Measure 3 cups juice, adding water if necessary. Discard pulp remaining in cheesecloth.

3. Place strained juice in a 6- to 8-quart heavy pot. Stir in pectin. Bring to a full rolling boil, stirring constantly. Stir in sugar. Return to a full rolling boil, stirring constantly. Boil hard 1 minute, stirring constantly. Remove from heat. Quickly skim off foam with a metal spoon.

4. Ladle hot jelly into hot, sterilized half-pint canning jars, leaving a ¼-inch headspace. Wipe jar rims; adjust lids and screw bands.

5. Process filled jars in a boiling-water canner 5 minutes (start timing when water returns to boiling). Remove jars from canner; cool on wire racks. **Makes 5 half-pint jars.**

PER 1 TABLESPOON: 61 cal., 0 g fat, 0 mg chol., 1 mg sodium, 15 g carb., 15 g sugars, 0 g fiber, 0 g pro.

✳ TEST KITCHEN TIP For sparkling clear jelly, be patient and resist the urge to press the juice through the cheesecloth. The clearest jelly is made from juice that drips through on its own.

PREP: 30 MINUTES   STAND: 30 MINUTES   COOK: 1 HOUR   PROCESS: 5 MINUTES

Apricot-Almond Spread

2 lb. fresh apricots, pitted and coarsely chopped (about 7¼ cups)

3 cups sugar

2 cups water

1 tsp. ground cinnamon

⅓ cup almond paste, crumbled

1 cup dried apricots, finely chopped

3 Tbsp. lemon juice

1 tsp. vanilla

1. In a large nonreactive bowl combine the fresh apricots, sugar, 1½ cups of the water, and the cinnamon. Cover and let stand 30 minutes, stirring occasionally. In a 6- to 8-quart heavy pot combine the remaining ½ cup water and the almond paste. Cook over medium-low heat until well combined, using a potato masher to break up almond paste as it heats.

2. Add apricot mixture and dried apricots to almond paste mixture in pot. Bring to boiling over medium heat, mashing with a potato masher as it cooks. Reduce heat; boil gently, uncovered, about 1 hour or until mixture is thick and mounds when stirred (bottom of pan should be visible when stirring), stirring frequently. Remove from heat. Stir in lemon juice and vanilla.

3. Ladle hot mixture into hot, sterilized half-pint canning jars, leaving a ¼-inch headspace. Wipe jar rims; adjust lids and screw bands.

4. Process filled jars in a boiling-water canner 5 minutes (start timing when water returns to boiling). Remove jars from canner; cool on wire racks. **Makes 6 half-pint jars.**

PER 1 TABLESPOON: 35 cal., 0 g fat, 0 mg chol., 0 mg sodium, 8 g carb., 8 g sugars, 0 g fiber, 0 g pro.

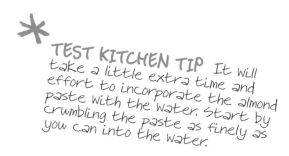

* TEST KITCHEN TIP It will take a little extra time and effort to incorporate the almond paste with the water. Start by crumbling the paste as finely as you can into the water.

For best texture and color, use bananas that are just ripe with a bright yellow color and no brown spots.

PREP: 20 MINUTES   **COOK:** 1 HOUR   **PROCESS:** 10 MINUTES

Apricot-Banana Jam

3 lb. fresh apricots, halved, pitted, and coarsely chopped (8¾ cups)

2 cups sugar

½ cup pure maple syrup

¼ cup water

2 medium bananas, coarsely mashed (⅔ cup)

3 Tbsp. lemon juice

1. In a 4- to 6-quart heavy pot combine apricots, sugar, maple syrup, and the water. Stir in bananas and lemon juice. Crush mixture with a potato masher. Bring to boiling, stirring frequently. Reduce heat; simmer, uncovered, 1 hour or until liquid has evaporated and mixture is thick, stirring occasionally. Remove from heat.

2. Ladle hot jam into hot, sterilized half-pint canning jars, leaving a ¼-inch headspace. Wipe jar rims; adjust lids and screw bands.

3. Process filled jars in a boiling-water canner 10 minutes (start timing when water returns to boiling). Remove jars from canner; cool on wire racks. **Makes 5 half-pint jars.**

PER 1 TABLESPOON: 35 cal., 0 g fat, 0 mg chol., 1 mg sodium, 9 g carb., 8 g sugars, 0 g fiber, 0 g pro.

* SIMPLY SERVE Make a twist on traditional s'mores with graham cracker squares, white chocolate, jam, and toasted marshmallows.

Tree-ripened peaches, available locally at farmers markets or from orchard stands, produce incomparably better jams than commercially produced fruits. Avoid peaches with any green, which indicates they were picked before they were ripe.

Peach Jam

7 cups sugar

4 cups finely chopped, peeled (see page 11) peaches (3 lb.)

¼ cup lemon juice

½ of a 6-oz. pkg. (1 foil pouch) liquid fruit pectin

1. In a 6- to 8-quart heavy pot combine sugar, peaches, and lemon juice. Bring to boiling over medium heat, stirring to dissolve sugar. Quickly stir in pectin. Bring to a full rolling boil, stirring constantly. Boil hard 1 minute, stirring constantly. Remove from heat. Quickly skim off foam with a metal spoon.

2. Ladle hot jam into hot, sterilized half-pint canning jars, leaving a ¼-inch headspace. Wipe jar rims; adjust lids and screw bands.

3. Process filled jars in a boiling-water canner 10 minutes (start timing when water returns to boiling). Remove jars from canner; cool on wire racks. **Makes 7 half-pint jars.**

CARDAMOM-PEACH JAM: Prepare as directed, except stir ¾ teaspoon freshly ground cardamom into the peach mixture after skimming off foam.

SWEET BASIL-PEACH JAM: Prepare as directed, except stir ½ cup snipped fresh basil into the peach mixture after skimming off foam.

BOURBON-PEACH JAM: Prepare as directed, except add ½ cup bourbon with the sugar, peaches, and lemon juice in Step 1.

CHIPOTLE-PEACH JAM: Prepare as directed, except add 2 finely chopped chipotle chile peppers in adobo sauce with the sugar, peaches, and lemon juice in Step 1.

PER 1 TABLESPOON PLAIN, CARDAMOM-PEACH, SWEET BASIL-PEACH, BOURBON-PEACH, AND CHIPOTLE-PEACH VARIATIONS: 54 cal., 0 g fat, 0 mg chol., 0 mg sodium, 14 g carb., 14 g sugars, 0 g fiber, 0 g pro.

Peach & Pepper Sriracha Jam

1 lime

6½ cups sugar

2 cups finely chopped, peeled (see page 11) peaches (1½ lb.)

¾ cup finely chopped red and/or yellow sweet pepper

2 Tbsp. sriracha sauce

½ of a 6-oz. pkg. (1 foil pouch) liquid fruit pectin

1. Remove 1 teaspoon zest and squeeze 2 tablespoons juice from lime. In a 6- to 8-quart heavy pot combine zest, juice, and the next 4 ingredients (through sriracha sauce). Bring to boiling, stirring constantly to dissolve sugar. Quickly stir in pectin. Bring to a full rolling boil, stirring constantly. Boil hard 1 minute, stirring constantly. Remove from heat. Quickly skim off foam with a metal spoon.

2. Ladle hot jam into hot, sterilized half-pint canning jars, leaving a ¼-inch headspace. Wipe jar rims; adjust lids and screw bands.

3. Process filled jars in a boiling-water canner 10 minutes (start timing when water returns to boiling). Remove jars from canner; cool on wire racks. **Makes 6 half-pint jars.**

PER 1 TABLESPOON: 57 cal., 0 g fat, 0 mg chol., 4 mg sodium, 15 g carb., 15 g sugars, 0 g fiber, 0 g pro.

✳ TEST KITCHEN TIP You can use a food processor to chop the peaches. Place small batches of cut-up, peeled peaches in the processor, and cover and pulse until peaches are finely chopped.

Champagne vinegar adds tang without overpowering tartness. If you can't find it, use white wine vinegar or white balsamic vinegar.

Peach Honey-Pistachio Conserve

5 cups chopped, peeled (see page 11) peaches (about 5 medium), or two 16-oz. pkg. frozen peach slices, partially thawed and chopped

1 cup honey

½ cup water

¼ cup champagne vinegar or white wine vinegar

2 cups sugar

1 cup snipped dried peaches or apricots

1 cup chopped pistachio nuts

½ tsp. ground cardamom

1. In a 6- to 8-quart nonreactive heavy pot combine chopped peaches, honey, the water, and vinegar. Bring to boiling; reduce heat. Simmer, covered, about 5 minutes or until peaches are tender, stirring occasionally. Use a potato masher to slightly crush peaches.

2. Stir sugar and dried peaches into peach mixture in pot. Return to boiling, stirring until sugar dissolves; reduce heat. Boil gently, uncovered, about 30 minutes or until mixture is syrupy, stirring occasionally. Remove from heat. Stir in pistachios and cardamom.

3. Ladle hot conserve into hot, sterilized half-pint canning jars, leaving a ¼-inch headspace. Wipe jar rims; adjust lids and screw bands.

4. Process filled jars in a boiling-water canner 5 minutes (start timing when water returns to boiling). Remove jars from canner; cool on wire racks. **Makes 6 half-pint jars.**

PER 1 TABLESPOON: 46 cal., 1 g fat, 0 mg chol., 7 mg sodium, 10 g carb., 9 g sugars, 0 g fiber, 0 g pro.

The unique flavor of saffron is impossible to duplicate. Saffron is the most expensive spice because of the labor-intensive harvesting method, but it is worth every penny.

Nectarine-Saffron Jam

7 cups sugar

4 cups finely chopped nectarines (2½ lb.)

¼ cup lemon juice

½ of a 6-oz. pkg. (1 foil pouch) liquid fruit pectin

Pinch saffron threads, crushed, or pinch ground saffron

1. In an 8- to 10-quart heavy pot combine sugar, nectarines, and lemon juice. Bring to a full rolling boil, stirring constantly to dissolve sugar. Quickly stir in pectin. Return to a full rolling boil, stirring constantly. Boil hard 1 minute, stirring constantly. Remove from heat. Quickly skim off foam with a metal spoon. Stir in saffron.

2. Ladle hot jam into hot, sterilized half-pint canning jars, leaving a ¼-inch headspace. Wipe jar rims; adjust lids and screw bands.

3. Process filled jars in a boiling-water canner 10 minutes (start timing when water returns to boiling). Remove jars from canner; cool on wire racks. **Makes 7 half-pint jars.**

PER 1 TABLESPOON: 68 cal., 0 g fat, 0 mg chol., 0 mg sodium, 18 g carb., 17 g sugars, 0 g fiber, 0 g pro.

Nectarine-Vanilla Bean Jam

3 lb. fresh nectarines, peeled (see page 11), pitted, and chopped (about 4 cups)

¼ cup lemon juice

2 vanilla beans, split lengthwise

7 cups sugar

½ of a 6-oz. pkg. (1 foil pouch) liquid fruit pectin

1. In a 6- to 8-quart heavy pot combine nectarines and lemon juice. Use a potato masher to crush nectarines to a pulp. Scrape the seeds from the vanilla bean pods (see page 218); add to pot. Stir in the vanilla bean pods and the sugar.

2. Bring mixture to boiling over medium heat, stirring constantly to dissolve sugar. Increase heat to medium-high; bring mixture to a full rolling boil, stirring constantly. Quickly stir in pectin. Return to a full rolling boil, stirring constantly. Boil hard 1 minute, stirring constantly. Remove from heat. Quickly skim off foam with a metal spoon. Remove and discard vanilla bean pods.

3. Ladle hot jam into hot, sterilized half-pint canning jars, leaving a ¼-inch headspace. Wipe jar rims; adjust lids and screw bands.

4. Process filled jars in a boiling-water canner 10 minutes (start timing when water returns to boiling). Remove jars from canner; cool on wire racks. **Makes 6 half-pint jars.**

PER 1 TABLESPOON: 65 cal., 0 g fat, 0 mg chol., 0 mg sodium, 17 g carb., 16 g sugars, 0 g fiber, 0 g pro.

TEST KITCHEN TIP Vanilla beans bring intense vanilla flavor to recipes. The tiny seeds are scraped out and added; the pods are steeped in hot liqwid and discarded. To remove the seeds, cut the pod lengthwise with a sharp paring knife and scrape out the seeds.

Plums are available in a spectrum of colors. For the deepest color, select dark purple plums. They will blend best with the dark color of balsamic vinegar.

Balsamic-Basil Plum Jam

- 6 cups finely chopped plums (4 lb.)
- ¼ cup water
- ¼ cup balsamic vinegar
- 1 1.75-oz. pkg. regular powdered fruit pectin or 6 Tbsp. classic powdered fruit pectin
- 8 cups sugar
- ⅓ cup chopped fresh basil

1. In a 6- to 8-quart heavy pot combine plums, the water, and vinegar. Stir in pectin. Bring to a full rolling boil, stirring constantly. Quickly stir in sugar. Return to a full rolling boil, stirring constantly. Boil hard 1 minute, stirring constantly. Remove from heat. Quickly skim off any foam with a metal spoon. Stir in basil.

2. Ladle hot jam into hot, sterilized half-pint canning jars, leaving a ¼-inch headspace. Wipe jar rims; adjust lids and screw bands.

3. Process filled jars in a boiling-water canner 10 minutes (start timing when water returns to boiling). Remove jars from canner; cool on wire racks. **Makes 13 half-pint jars.**

PER 1 TABLESPOON: 39 cal., 0 g fat, 0 mg chol., 0 mg sodium, 10 g carb., 10 g sugars, 0 g fiber, 0 g pro.

*

SIMPLY SERVE Liven up a grilling party by topping flatbread with soft goat cheese, chopped grilled plums, a generous drizzle of this tangy plum jam, and fresh arugula.

Toasted Walnut-Plum Conserve

5 cups finely chopped ripe purple plums (1¾ to 2 lb.)

1 cup water

3 Tbsp. lemon juice

3 cups sugar

1 cup finely chopped pitted dried plums (prunes)

1½ cups chopped toasted walnuts

1. In a 4- to 6-quart heavy pot combine fresh plums, the water, and lemon juice. Using a potato masher, lightly crush plums. Bring to boiling; reduce heat. Simmer, covered, about 5 minutes or until plums are tender, stirring occasionally. Stir in sugar and dried plums.

2. Return to boiling, stirring to dissolve sugar; reduce heat. Simmer, uncovered, about 20 minutes or until mixture is thickened, stirring occasionally. Remove from heat. Stir in walnuts.*

3. Ladle hot conserve into hot, sterilized half-pint canning jars, leaving a ¼-inch headspace. Wipe jar rims; adjust lids and screw bands.

4. Process filled jars in a boiling-water canner 10 minutes (start timing when water returns to boiling). Remove jars from canner; cool on wire racks. **Makes 6 half-pint jars.**

*NOTE: If you prefer, sprinkle the toasted walnuts over the conserve at serving time instead of stirring them in before processing.

PER 2 TABLESPOONS: 89 cal., 2 g fat, 0 mg chol., 0 mg sodium, 17 g carb., 16 g sugars, 1 g fiber, 1 g pro.

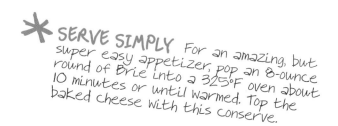

* SERVE SIMPLY For an amazing, but super easy appetizer, pop an 8-ounce round of Brie into a 325°F oven about 10 minutes or until warmed. Top the baked cheese with this conserve.

CHAPTER 3

From the Orchard

Cider 'n' Spice Jelly

5   cups fresh-pressed apple
    cider

2   cinnamon sticks, broken

8   whole allspice

8   whole cloves

7½ cups sugar

½   of a 6-oz. pkg. (1 foil
    pouch) liquid fruit pectin

1. In a 6- to 8-quart nonreactive heavy pot combine the first four ingredients (through cloves). Bring to boiling; reduce heat to medium-low. Simmer, covered, 20 minutes. Line a sieve with a double layer of 100-percent-cotton cheesecloth; place sieve over a large bowl. Strain cider mixture through cheesecloth. If desired, reserve spices to add to canning jars.

2. Wash the pot, then return strained cider to pot. Stir in sugar. Bring to a full rolling boil, stirring constantly. Add pectin. Return to a full rolling boil, stirring constantly. Boil hard 1 minute, stirring constantly. Remove from heat.

3. Ladle hot jelly into hot, sterilized half-pint canning jars, leaving a ¼-inch headspace. If desired, add some of the reserved cinnamon, allspice, and cloves to each jar. Wipe jar rims; adjust lids and screw bands.

4. Process filled jars in a boiling-water canner 5 minutes (start timing when water returns to boiling). Remove jars from canner; cool on wire racks. **Makes 7 half-pint jars.**

PER 1 TABLESPOON: 57 cal., 0 g fat, 0 mg chol., 0 mg sodium, 14 g carb., 13 g sugars, 0 g fiber, 0 g pro.

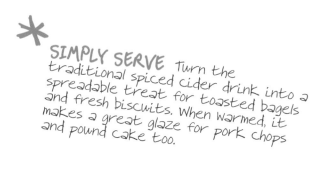

* SIMPLY SERVE Turn the traditional spiced cider drink into a spreadable treat for toasted bagels and fresh biscuits. When warmed, it makes a great glaze for pork chops and pound cake too.

Apple-Blueberry Jelly

3 lb. Granny Smith apples (about 9 medium)

5 cups fresh blueberries (2 lb.)

3 cups water

3 cups sugar

1. Coarsely chop the apples (do not peel or core). Place blueberries in a 10-quart heavy pot; crush slightly with a potato masher. Add apples and the water to blueberries in pot. Bring to boiling. Boil gently, uncovered, 20 minutes, stirring occasionally.

2. Line a large colander with a double layer of 100-percent-cotton cheesecloth; place over a large bowl. Pour apple mixture into colander. Let stand about 30 minutes or until juices stop dripping (avoid squeezing juice from cheesecloth; this can cause cloudy jelly). Measure 4 cups juice. Discard fruit.

3. In the same pot combine apple-blueberry juice and the sugar. Bring to a full rolling boil, stirring to dissolve sugar. Boil hard, uncovered, about 15 minutes or until jelly sheets off of a metal spoon and reaches 220°F. Remove pot from heat. Quickly skim off foam with a metal spoon.

4. Ladle hot jelly into hot, sterilized half-pint canning jars, leaving a ¼-inch headspace. Wipe jar rims; adjust lids and screw bands.

5. Process filled jars in a boiling-water canner 5 minutes (start timing when water returns to boiling). Remove jars from canner; cool on wire racks until set. **Makes 3 half-pint jars.**

PER 1 TABLESPOON: 75 cal., 0 g fat, 0 mg chol., 1 mg sodium, 20 g carb., 18 g sugars, 1 g fiber, 0 g pro.

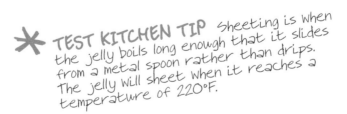

✳ TEST KITCHEN TIP Sheeting is when the jelly boils long enough that it slides from a metal spoon rather than drips. The jelly will sheet when it reaches a temperature of 220°F.

The classic flavor combo of apple and caramel comes together in this candylike jam. The brown sugar and vanilla turn a simple apple jam into a true delight.

Caramel Apple Jam

4 lb. tart apples (about 12 medium), such as Granny Smith, cored and chopped

1¼ cups water

2 Tbsp. lemon juice

3 cups granulated sugar

1 cup packed brown sugar

1 Tbsp. butter

1 Tbsp. vanilla

1. In a large saucepan combine apples, ½ cup of the water, and the lemon juice. Bring mixture to boiling over medium-high heat, stirring constantly; reduce heat. Simmer, covered, 25 to 30 minutes or until apples are very tender, stirring frequently. Press apples through a food mill or sieve until you have 5 cups pulp; discard skins.

2. Meanwhile, for caramel, pour granulated sugar into a 6- to 8-quart heavy pot, spreading evenly. Heat over medium-high heat until sugar begins to melt, shaking pot occasionally; do not stir. When the sugar starts to melt, reduce heat to medium-low and cook 5 to 10 minutes or until all of the sugar is melted and golden, stirring as necessary with a wooden spoon. Remove from heat. Carefully add the remaining ¾ cup water (caramel will spatter and become hard). Return to heat; cook and stir over medium heat until caramel melts.

3. Carefully add the 5 cups apple pulp and the brown sugar to caramel (caramel will spatter and become hard). Cook over medium heat until brown sugar is dissolved and caramel melts, stirring constantly. Increase heat to medium-high. Boil gently, uncovered, about 10 minutes or until mixture is thickened, stirring frequently. Remove from heat. Stir in butter and vanilla.

4. Ladle hot jam into hot, sterilized half-pint canning jars, leaving a ¼-inch headspace. Wipe jar rims; adjust lids and screw bands.

5. Process filled jars in a boiling-water canner 10 minutes (start timing when water returns to boiling). Remove jars from canner; cool on wire racks. **Makes 6 half-pint jars.**

PER 1 TABLESPOON: 57 cal., 0 g fat, 0 mg chol., 3 mg sodium, 14 g carb., 13 g sugars, 1 g fiber, 0 g pro.

The peak season for apples varies by region. Visit local orchards often to find freshly harvested fruits. Supermarkets carry the best apples in September and October.

Dutch Apple Preserves

1 lb. tart green apples (about 3 medium), peeled, cored, and coarsely chopped

1¼ cups apple juice

½ cup raisins

2 Tbsp. lemon juice

2 cups granulated sugar

1½ tsp. apple pie spice

1 1.75-oz. pkg. powdered fruit pectin for low-sugar recipes or 3 Tbsp. powdered fruit pectin for low- or no-sugar recipes

1 cup packed brown sugar

1. In a 6- to 8-quart pot combine the first four ingredients (through lemon juice). In a bowl stir together ¼ cup of the granulated sugar, the apple pie spice, and pectin. Stir into apple mixture. Bring to a full rolling boil over high heat, stirring constantly. Stir in the remaining 1¾ cups granulated sugar and the brown sugar. Return to a full rolling boil, stirring constantly. Boil hard 1 minute, stirring constantly. Remove from heat. Quickly skim off any foam with a metal spoon.

2. Ladle hot preserves into hot, sterilized half-pint canning jars, leaving a ¼-inch headspace. Wipe jar rims; adjust lids and screw bands.

3. Process filled jars in a boiling-water canner 10 minutes (start timing when water returns to boiling). Remove jars from canner; cool on wire racks. **Makes 4 half-pint jars.**

PER 1 TABLESPOON: 54 cal., 0 g fat, 0 mg chol., 2 mg sodium, 14 g carb., 13 g sugars, 0 g fiber, 0 g pro.

Apple-Cherry Chutney

3 lb. apples, peeled, cored, and chopped (8 cups)

1½ cups dried tart red cherries

2 cups packed brown sugar

2 cups cider vinegar

1 cup chopped sweet onion

1 cup chopped red sweet pepper

2 tsp. ground cardamom

½ tsp. salt

1. In a 6- to 8-quart heavy pot stir together all ingredients. Bring to boiling; reduce heat. Simmer, uncovered, about 1 hour or until thickened, stirring occasionally.

2. Ladle hot chutney into hot, sterilized half-pint canning jars, leaving a ½-inch headspace. Wipe jar rims; adjust lids and screw bands.

3. Process filled jars in a boiling-water canner 10 minutes (start timing when water returns to boiling). Remove jars from canner; cool on wire racks. **Makes 7 half-pint jars.**

PER 2 TABLESPOONS: 76 cal., 0 g fat, 0 mg chol., 31 mg sodium, 19 g carb., 17 g sugars, 1 g fiber, 0 g pro.

* SERVE SIMPLY This robust, savory chutney has just a hint of cardamom flavor. Slather it on marble rye to make an extraordinary homemade chicken salad sandwich.

Lower Sugar

This Thai-inspired fruit spread can be spicy or mild, depending on the red curry paste you select. Look for this unique ingredient with the Asian foods at the supermarket.

Curry-Coconut Apple Butter

4½ lb. tart cooking apples, cored and quartered (about 14 medium)

3 cups apple cider or apple juice

2 cups sugar

2 Tbsp. lime juice

2 Tbsp. red curry paste

½ cup unsweetened canned coconut milk

1. In an 8- to 10-quart heavy pot combine apples and cider. Bring to boiling; reduce heat. Simmer, covered, 30 minutes, stirring occasionally. Press apples through a food mill or sieve until you have 7½ cups pulp; discard skins. Return pulp to pot.

2. Stir in sugar, lime juice, and curry paste. Bring to boiling; reduce heat. Cook, uncovered, over low to medium-low heat about 2½ hours or until very thick and mixture mounds on a spoon, stirring frequently. Stir in coconut milk; heat through.

3. Ladle hot apple butter into hot, sterilized half-pint canning jars, leaving a ¼-inch headspace. Wipe jar rims; adjust lids and screw bands.

4. Process filled jars in a boiling-water canner 5 minutes (start timing when water returns to boiling). Remove jars from canner; cool on wire racks. **Makes 5 half-pint jars.**

PER 1 TABLESPOON: 39 cal., 0 g fat, 0 mg chol., 11 mg sodium, 9 g carb., 8 g sugars, 1 g fiber, 1 g pro.

* SERVE SIMPLY Turn up the heat on basic grilled chicken kabob wraps by smearing this sweet and hot spread on soft flatbreads.

Pear Pepper-Mint Jelly

2¼ lb. ripe pears, coarsely chopped (do not core or peel)

1⅓ cups water

2 Tbsp. whole black peppercorns

¼ tsp. ground white pepper

3½ cups sugar

9 6- to 7-inch sprigs fresh mint

½ of a 6-oz. pkg. (1 foil pouch) liquid fruit pectin

2 Tbsp. lemon juice

1. In a 6- to 8-quart heavy pot combine the first four ingredients (through white pepper). Bring to boiling. Boil gently, covered, 20 minutes, stirring occasionally.

2. Line a large colander with a double layer of 100-percent-cotton cheesecloth. Place colander over a large bowl. Pour pear mixture into colander. Let stand about 30 minutes or until juices stop dripping. Gather up the cheesecloth and gently squeeze out juice from the pears. Measure out 1¾ cups juice. If you have extra juice, save for another use. If you don't have enough juice, add as much water as you need to make 1¾ cups.

3. Using 100-percent-cotton string, tie mint sprigs in a bundle. In the same pot combine the pear juice, sugar, and mint. Bring to boiling, stirring to dissolve sugar. Quickly stir in pectin and lemon juice. Bring to a full rolling boil, stirring constantly. Boil hard 1 minute, stirring constantly. Remove from heat. Quickly skim off any foam with a metal spoon. Remove and discard mint bundle and any stray mint leaves.

4. Ladle hot jelly into hot, sterilized half-pint canning jars, leaving a ¼-inch headspace. Wipe jar rims; adjust lids and screw bands.

5. Process filled jars in a boiling-water canner 5 minutes (start timing when water returns to boiling). Remove jars from canner; cool on wire racks until set. **Makes 3 half-pint jars.**

PER 1 TABLESPOON: 58 cal., 0 g fat, 0 mg chol., 0 mg sodium, 15 g carb., 14 g sugars, 1 g fiber, 0 g pro.

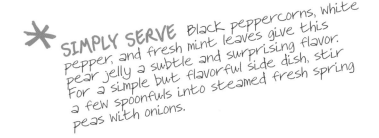

* SIMPLY SERVE Black peppercorns, white pepper, and fresh mint leaves give this pear jelly a subtle and surprising flavor. For a simple but flavorful side dish, stir a few spoonfuls into steamed fresh spring peas with onions.

Vanilla-Caramel Pear Butter

4½ lb. ripe pears, cored and quartered

3 cups pear nectar and/or apple juice

2 cups packed brown sugar

1 Tbsp. lemon juice

1 Tbsp. vanilla

1. In an 8- to 10-quart heavy pot combine pears and nectar. Bring to boiling; reduce heat. Simmer, covered, 1 hour, stirring occasionally. Coarsely mash pears with a potato masher. Press pears through a food mill or a fine-mesh sieve until you have 8 cups pulp; discard skins. Return pulp to pot.

2. Stir in remaining ingredients. Bring to boiling; reduce heat. Cook, uncovered, over low heat 1½ to 2 hours or until very thick and mixture mounds on a spoon, stirring frequently.

3. Ladle hot pear butter into hot, sterilized half-pint canning jars, leaving a ¼-inch headspace. Wipe jar rims; adjust lids and screw bands.

4. Process filled jars in a boiling water canner 5 minutes (start timing when water returns to boiling). Remove jars from canner; cool on wire racks. **Makes 4 half-pint jars.**

PER 1 TABLESPOON: 59 cal., 0 g fat, 0 mg chol., 3 mg sodium, 15 g carb., 13 g sugars, 1 g fiber, 0 g pro.

✳ SIMPLY SERVE This richly flavored pear butter has the perfect consistency to use as a filling for pastries and stuffed French toast or to spoon over ice cream.

PREP: 20 MINUTES   **COOK:** 1 HOUR   **PROCESS:** 10 MINUTES

Pear-Fig Chutney

4   to 5 medium ripe pears,
    peeled, cored, and
    chopped (4 cups)

2   cups cider vinegar

2   cups packed brown sugar

1   cup chopped red onion

1   cup chopped dried figs

4   cloves garlic, minced

1   Tbsp. apple pie spice

1   tsp. salt

1. In a 4- to 6-quart heavy pot stir together all ingredients. Bring to boiling; reduce heat. Simmer, uncovered, about 1 hour or until thickened and most of the liquid has evaporated, stirring occasionally.

2. Ladle hot chutney into hot, sterilized 4-ounce canning jars, leaving a ½-inch headspace. Wipe jar rims; adjust lids and screw bands.

3. Process filled jars in a boiling-water canner 10 minutes (start timing when water returns to boiling). Remove jars from canner; cool on wire racks. **Makes seven 4-ounce jars.**

PER 1 TABLESPOON: 53 cal., 0 g fat, 0 mg chol., 52 mg sodium, 13 g carb., 12 g sugars, 1 g fiber, 0 g pro.

* TEST KITCHEN TIP Use golden Calimyrna figs or dark Mission figs. The variety you choose will determine the color of your chutney.

Pear-Raspberry Jam with Rosemary

- 2 lemons
- 3 medium ripe pears, peeled, cored, and chopped (3 cups)
- 2 cups fresh raspberries, crushed
- 4 sprigs fresh rosemary
- 1 1.75-oz. pkg. regular powdered fruit pectin or 6 Tbsp. classic powdered fruit pectin
- 5 cups sugar

1. Finely shred 2 teaspoons zest and squeeze ¼ cup juice from lemons. In a 4- to 6-quart heavy pot combine lemon zest, lemon juice, and the next four ingredients (through pectin). Bring to a full rolling boil, stirring constantly. Stir in sugar. Return to a full rolling boil, stirring constantly. Boil hard 1 minute, stirring constantly. Remove from heat. Quickly skim off foam with a metal spoon. Use tongs to remove and discard rosemary sprigs.

2. Ladle hot jam into hot, sterilized half-pint canning jars, leaving a ¼-inch headspace. Wipe jar rims; adjust lids and screw bands.

3. Process filled jars in a boiling-water canner 10 minutes (start timing when water returns to boiling). Remove jars from canner; cool on wire racks. **Makes 6 half-pint jars.**

PER 1 TABLESPOON: 53 cal., 0 g fat, 0 mg chol., 0 mg sodium, 13 g carb., 13 g sugars, 0 g fiber, 0 g pro.

✳ SIMPLY SERVE Instead of honey, spread some of this pale pink jam on oven-fresh corn muffins or squares of corn bread. Or make it the star in the centers of nutty thumbprint cookies.

CHAPTER 4

Citrus Fresh

This spunky marmalade gets its intense flavor from the combination of crystallized ginger and ginger juice. Look for crystallized ginger in the spice section and ginger juice in the health aisle of your supermarket.

Gingered Orange Marmalade

14 to 16 large oranges (8 to 10 lb.)

2½ cups water

⅛ tsp. baking soda

1 cup coarsely snipped crystallized ginger

2 Tbsp. ginger juice

4 cups sugar

1 1.75-oz. pkg. powdered fruit pectin for lower-sugar recipes or 3 Tbsp. powdered fruit pectin for low- or no-sugar recipes

1. Use a paring knife to score the peels of five or six of the oranges into four lengthwise sections; remove peels. Scrape off white portions of peels; discard. Cut peels into very thin strips; measure 1 cup orange peel strips.

2. Cut off slices from both ends of all the oranges. Cut away the peels (if present) and white parts, working from the tops to the bottoms. Working over a bowl to catch juice, remove fruit sections by cutting between a section and the membrane. Cut back between the section and the next membrane to release the section (see page 103). Repeat. You should have about 4 cups orange sections with their juice.

3. In a large saucepan combine orange peel strips, the water, and baking soda. Bring to boiling; reduce heat. Simmer, covered, 20 minutes, stirring occasionally. Stir in orange sections and their juice, crystallized ginger, and ginger juice. Simmer, uncovered, 10 minutes more. Measure 5½ cups of the orange mixture; discard any remaining mixture.

4. Transfer the 5½ cups orange mixture to a 6- to 8-quart heavy pot. In a bowl stir together ¼ cup of the sugar and the pectin; stir into orange mixture. Bring to a full rolling boil, stirring constantly. Quickly stir in the remaining 3¾ cups sugar. Return to a full rolling boil, stirring constantly. Boil hard 1 minute, stirring constantly. Remove from heat. Quickly skim off foam with a metal spoon.

5. Ladle hot marmalade into hot, sterilized half-pint canning jars, leaving a ¼-inch headspace. Wipe jar rims; adjust lids and screw bands.

6. Process filled jars in a boiling-water canner 5 minutes (start timing when water returns to boiling). Remove jars from canner; cool on wire racks. **Makes 8 half-pint jars.**

PER 1 TABLESPOON: 51 cal., 0 g fat, 0 mg chol., 3 mg sodium, 13 g carb., 11 g sugars, 1 g fiber, 0 g pro.

Blood oranges are very juicy and have a wonderful berrylike flavor. Find these red-flesh oranges—especially Moro, the darkest red variety—in the grocery store from December to March.

Blood Orange-Vanilla Bean Jelly

2 cups freshly squeezed blood orange juice or orange juice

⅓ cup freshly squeezed lemon juice

⅔ cup water

1 1.75-oz. pkg. regular powdered fruit pectin or 6 Tbsp. classic powdered fruit pectin

1 small vanilla bean

3½ cups sugar

1. Pour orange juice through a fine-mesh sieve into a liquid measuring cup; discard pulp. Measure 2 cups juice, adding water if necessary. Transfer the orange juice to a 6- to 8-quart heavy pot. Pour lemon juice through the sieve into pot; discard pulp. Stir in the ⅔ cup water and the pectin.

2. Split vanilla bean in half lengthwise. Use the tip of a paring knife to scrape out the seeds (see page 218). Add vanilla seeds to juice mixture, whisking to distribute seeds evenly. Bring to a full rolling boil, stirring constantly. Stir in sugar. Return to a full rolling boil, stirring constantly. Boil hard 1 minute, stirring constantly. Remove from heat. Quickly skim off foam with a metal spoon.

3. Ladle hot jelly into hot, sterilized half-pint canning jars, leaving a ¼-inch headspace. Wipe jar rims; adjust lids and screw bands.

4. Process filled jars in a boiling-water canner 5 minutes (start timing when water returns to boiling). Remove jars from canner; cool on wire racks. **Makes 4 half-pint jars.**

PER 1 TABLESPOON: 61 cal., 0 g fat, 0 mg chol., 2 mg sodium, 16 g carb., 14 g sugars, 0 g fiber, 0 g pro.

* SIMPLY SERVE Drizzle this ruby red jelly over vanilla bean ice cream and top with fresh orange segments for a knockout dessert.

Orange & Fennel Marmalade

8 to 10 large oranges (about 6½ lb.)

1¾ cups water

⅛ tsp. baking soda

1 cup finely chopped fennel bulb

4 cups sugar

1 1.75-oz. pkg. powdered fruit pectin for lower-sugar recipes or 3 Tbsp. powdered fruit pectin for low- or no-sugar recipes

1 Tbsp. snipped fresh thyme

1. Use a vegetable peeler to remove the peels from three or four of the oranges, avoiding the white pith underneath. Cut peels into very thin strips; measure ¾ cup peel strips.

2. Cut off slices from both ends of all of the oranges. Cut away any remaining peel and any white portions on the oranges. Working over a bowl to catch juice, section oranges. You should have about 3½ cups orange sections with their juice.

3. In a large saucepan combine orange peel strips, the water, and the baking soda. Bring to boiling; reduce heat. Simmer, covered, 20 minutes, stirring occasionally. Stir in orange sections, any juices, and fennel. Simmer, uncovered, 10 minutes more. Measure 5½ cups of the orange mixture. Discard any excess mixture.

4. Transfer the 5½ cups orange mixture to a 6- to 8-quart heavy pot. In a bowl stir together ¼ cup of the sugar and the pectin; stir into orange mixture. Bring to a full rolling boil, stirring constantly. Quickly stir in the remaining sugar. Return to a full rolling boil, stirring constantly. Boil hard 1 minute, stirring constantly. Remove from heat. Quickly skim off foam with a metal spoon. Stir in fresh thyme.

5. Ladle hot marmalade into hot, sterilized half-pint canning jars, leaving a ¼-inch headspace. Wipe jar rims; adjust lids and screw bands.

6. Process filled jars in a boiling-water canner 10 minutes (start timing when water returns to boiling). Remove jars from canner; cool on wire racks. **Makes 7 half-pint jars.**

PER 1 TABLESPOON: 35 cal., 0 g fat, 0 mg chol., 2 mg sodium, 9 g carb., 8 g sugars, 0 g fiber, 0 g pro.

★TEST KITCHEN TIP To section citrus fruit, hold it over a bowl if the recipe says to catch juices. Tip the fruit to its side and cut into the center between one section and the membrane. Cut along the other side of the section next to membrane to free the section.

Clementine Jelly

2 cups fresh clementine juice

¼ cup fresh lemon juice

3½ cups sugar

½ of a 6-oz. pkg. (1 foil pouch) liquid fruit pectin

1. In a 6- to 8-quart heavy pot stir together the juices and sugar. Bring to a full rolling boil, stirring constantly. Stir in pectin. Boil hard 1 minute, stirring constantly. Remove from heat. Quickly skim off foam with a metal spoon.

2. Ladle hot jelly into hot, sterilized half-pint canning jars, leaving a ¼-inch headspace. Wipe jar rims; adjust lids and screw bands.

3. Process filled jars in a boiling-water canner 5 minutes (start timing when water returns to boiling). Remove jars from canner; cool on wire racks. **Makes 4 half-pint jars.**

PER 1 TABLESPOON: 47 cal., 0 g fat, 0 mg chol., 0 mg sodium, 12 g carb., 12 g sugars, 0 g fiber, 0 g pro.

★ TEST KITCHEN TIP Choose clementines that feel heavy and firm. You will need about 15 of these small fruits to get 2 cups of juice.

When your herb garden is bursting with fresh lavender in the summer, pick the just-opened purple blossoms to make this golden jelly.

Lemon-Lavender Jelly

3 to 4 medium lemons

1⅓ cups boiling water

2 Tbsp. fresh lavender flowers or 1 Tbsp. dried lavender flowers, lightly crushed

4¼ cups sugar

½ of a 6-oz. pkg. (1 foil pouch) liquid fruit pectin

1. Remove 2 tablespoons zest and squeeze ¾ cup juice from lemons. In a bowl combine the lemon zest, lemon juice, the boiling water, and lavender flowers. Let stand 20 minutes. Strain mixture through a fine-mesh sieve. Discard peel, pulp, and flowers.

2. In a 6- to 8-quart heavy pot combine lemon juice mixture and the sugar. Bring to a full rolling boil, stirring constantly. Stir in pectin. Return to a full rolling boil, stirring constantly. Boil hard 1 minute, stirring constantly. Remove from heat. Quickly skim off foam with a metal spoon.

3. Ladle hot jelly into hot, sterilized half-pint canning jars, leaving a ¼-inch headspace. Wipe jar rims; adjust lids and screw bands.

4. Process filled jars in a boiling-water canner 5 minutes (start timing when water returns to boiling). Remove jars; cool on wire racks. **Makes 4 half-pint jars.**

PER 1 TABLESPOON: 56 cal., 0 g fat, 0 mg chol., 0 mg sodium, 14 g carb., 14 g sugars, 0 g fiber, 0 g pro.

Raspberry Lemonade Jelly

5 lemons

2 cups raspberries

½ cup water

4¼ cups sugar

½ of a 6-oz. pkg. (1 foil pouch) liquid fruit pectin

1. Remove 3 tablespoons lemon zest and squeeze ¾ cup juice from lemons. In a small saucepan slightly crush raspberries. Stir in the ½ cup water and the lemon zest. Bring to boiling; reduce heat. Simmer, uncovered, 5 minutes. Remove from heat; let stand 10 minutes. Line a fine-mesh sieve with two layers of 100-percent-cotton cheesecloth; set sieve over a medium bowl. Pour raspberry mixture into sieve. Let stand 10 minutes to allow juices to drain. Using the back of a spoon, press gently to extract any remaining liquid; discard seeds and peel. Measure raspberry juice and add enough water to equal 1⅓ cups total liquid.

2. In a 6- to 8-quart heavy pot combine raspberry juice, lemon juice, and sugar. Bring to a full rolling boil, stirring constantly. Stir in pectin. Return to a full rolling boil, stirring constantly. Boil hard 1 minute, stirring constantly. Remove from heat. Skim off foam with a metal spoon.

3. Ladle hot jelly into hot, sterilized half-pint canning jars, leaving a ¼-inch headspace. Wipe jar rims; adjust lids and screw bands.

4. Process filled jars in a boiling-water canner 5 minutes (start timing when water returns to boiling). Remove jars; cool on wire racks. **Makes 4 half-pint jars.**

PER 1 TABLESPOON: 55 cal., 0 g fat, 0 mg chol., 0 mg sodium, 14 g carb., 14 g sugars, 0 g fiber, 0 g pro.

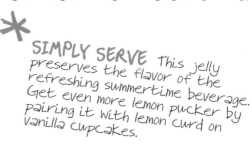

* SIMPLY SERVE This jelly preserves the flavor of the refreshing summertime beverage. Get even more lemon pucker by pairing it with lemon curd on vanilla cupcakes.

Meyer lemons, a cross between an orange and a lemon, are smaller than regular lemons and much sweeter. Regular lemons are available year-round, but your best bet for finding Meyers is from December through May.

Lemon-Lime-Orange Marmalade

3 medium oranges

1 medium Meyer lemon

1 medium lime

1½ cups water

⅛ tsp. baking soda

5 cups sugar

½ of a 6-oz. pkg. (1 foil pouch) liquid fruit pectin

1. Use a paring knife to score the peels of the oranges, lemon, and lime into four lengthwise sections; remove peels. Scrape off white portions of peels; discard. Cut peels into thin strips. In a large saucepan bring peels, the water, and baking soda to boiling. Cover; simmer 20 minutes. Do not drain.

2. Meanwhile, working over a bowl to catch juice, remove fruit sections by cutting between a section and the membrane. Cut back between the section and the next membrane to release the section (see page 103). Repeat until all fruits are sectioned. Add sections and juices to saucepan; return to boiling. Cover and simmer 10 minutes (you should have 3 cups fruit mixture).

3. In an 8- to 10-quart heavy pot combine fruit mixture and sugar. Bring to a full rolling boil, stirring constantly. Quickly stir in pectin. Return to a full rolling boil. Boil hard 1 minute, stirring constantly. Remove from heat. Quickly skim off foam with a metal spoon.

4. Ladle marmalade into hot, sterilized half-pint canning jars, leaving a ¼-inch headspace. Wipe jar rims; adjust lids and screw bands.

5. Process filled jars in a boiling-water canner 5 minutes (start timing when water returns to boiling). Remove jars; cool on wire racks. Allow jars to stand at room temperature at least 1 week for marmalade to set. **Makes 5 half-pint jars.**

PER 1 TABLESPOON: 52 cal., 0 g fat, 0 mg chol., 2 mg sodium, 13 g carb., 13 g sugars, 0 g fiber, 0 g pro.

When you taste this translucent light green jelly, envision a margarita dancing with a piña colada. The flavors are delicate with just a hint of coconut.

Key Lime-Coconut Jelly

18 to 20 Key limes or 6 Persian limes

1¾ cups coconut water

4 cups sugar

½ of a 6-oz. pkg. (1 foil pouch) liquid fruit pectin

½ tsp. coconut extract

1 drop green food coloring

1. Remove 2 tablespoons zest and squeeze ¾ cup juice from limes. In a bowl combine lime zest, lime juice, and coconut water; let stand 5 minutes. Line a fine-mesh sieve with two layers of 100-percent-cotton cheesecloth; set sieve over a medium bowl. Pour lime mixture into sieve. Let stand 10 minutes to allow juices to drain. Using the back of a spoon, press lime zest gently to extract any remaining liquid; discard zest. Measure lime juice mixture, adding enough water to equal 2½ cups total liquid.

2. In a 4- to 6-quart pot combine lime juice mixture and sugar. Bring to a full rolling boil, stirring constantly. Quickly stir in pectin. Return to a full rolling boil, stirring constantly. Boil hard 1 minute, stirring constantly. Remove from heat. Stir in coconut extract and food coloring. Quickly skim off foam with a metal spoon.

3. Ladle hot jelly into hot, sterilized half-pint canning jars, leaving a ¼-inch headspace. Wipe jar rims; adjust lids and screw bands.

4. Process filled jars in a boiling-water canner 5 minutes (start timing when water returns to boiling). Remove jars from canner; cool on wire racks. **Makes 4 half-pint jars.**

PER 1 TABLESPOON: 47 cal., 0 g fat, 0 mg chol., 2 mg sodium, 12 g carb., 12 g sugars, 0 g fiber, 0 g pro.

Ruby Red Grapefruit Jelly

4 cups sugar

2 cups red grapefruit juice

2 Tbsp. lemon juice

½ of a 6-oz. pkg. (1 foil pouch) liquid fruit pectin

1. In a 5- to 6-quart heavy pot combine sugar, grapefruit juice, and lemon juice. Bring to a full rolling boil, stirring constantly. Stir in pectin. Return to a full rolling boil, stirring constantly. Boil hard 1 minute, stirring constantly. Remove from heat. Quickly skim off foam with a metal spoon.

2. Ladle hot jelly into hot, sterilized half-pint canning jars, leaving a ¼-inch headspace. Wipe jar rims; adjust lids and screw bands.

3. Process filled jars in a boiling-water canner 5 minutes (start timing when water returns to boiling). Remove jars from canner; cool on wire racks. **Makes 5 half-pint jars.**

PER 1 TABLESPOON: 50 cal., 0 g fat, 0 mg chol., 0 mg sodium, 13 g carb., 13 g sugars, 0 g fiber, 0 g pro.

SIMPLY SERVE This jewel-tone jelly adds sparkle to pound cake. Spoon it over cake topped with fresh grapefruit segments and raspberries.

CHAPTER 5

Tropical Treasures

If you love sweet-and-sour stir-fry, try this bright red jelly for a simple sweet and hot sauce. Lightly brush the jelly on grilled poppers for additional sweet heat.

Peppery Papaya Jelly

2 lb. fresh papayas

1 cup red wine vinegar

1 medium fresh banana chile pepper, stemmed, seeded, and coarsely chopped*

1 small fresh habañero chile pepper or other orange or red hot chile pepper, stemmed, seeded, and coarsely chopped*

5 cups sugar

½ of a 6-oz. pkg. (1 foil pouch) liquid fruit pectin

1. Halve papayas; scoop out and discard seeds. Peel and cut up papayas; add pieces to a food processor. Cover and process until smooth.

2. Transfer pureed papaya to a medium nonreactive saucepan. Add vinegar, banana pepper, and habañero pepper. Bring to boiling, stirring constantly. Reduce heat; simmer, covered, 5 minutes, stirring occasionally. Strain mixture through a sieve, pressing with the back of a spoon to remove all the liquid; discard pulp. Measure 3 cups liquid.

3. In a 6-quart heavy pot combine the 3 cups liquid and the sugar. Bring to a full rolling boil, stirring constantly. Quickly stir in pectin. Return to a full rolling boil, stirring constantly. Boil hard 1 minute, stirring constantly. Remove from heat. Quickly skim off foam with a metal spoon.

4. Ladle hot jelly into hot, sterilized half-pint canning jars, leaving a ¼-inch headspace. Wipe jar rims; adjust lids and screw bands.

5. Process filled jars in a boiling-water canner 5 minutes (start timing when water returns to boiling). Remove jars from canner; cool on wire racks. **Makes 5 half-pint jars.**

PER 1 TABLESPOON: 48 cal., 0 g fat, 0 mg chol., 1 mg sodium, 12 g carb., 12 g sugars, 0 g fiber, 0 g pro.

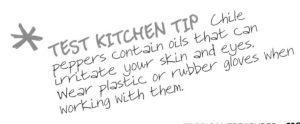

* TEST KITCHEN TIP Chile peppers contain oils that can irritate your skin and eyes. Wear plastic or rubber gloves when working with them.

Banana-Passion Fruit Spread

15 to 20 medium ripe orange or yellow passion fruits (about 2¼ lb.)

6 medium bananas, sliced*

5 cups sugar

½ cup plain coconut water

2 Tbsp. lemon juice

1 6-oz. pkg. (2 pouches) liquid fruit pectin

1. Cut passion fruits in half. Scoop pulp and seeds into a 6- to 8-quart heavy pot. You should have about 2 cups pulp and seeds. Bring to boiling; remove from heat. Cool slightly; strain half of the pulp and seeds through a fine-mesh sieve or a food mill; discard seeds. Return the strained pulp to the pot with the remaining pulp and seeds. Add sliced bananas. Mash bananas with a potato masher. Stir in sugar, coconut water, and lemon juice.

2. Bring to boiling over medium heat, stirring to dissolve sugar. Quickly stir in pectin. Bring to a full rolling boil, stirring constantly. Boil hard 1 minute, stirring constantly. Remove from heat. Quickly skim off foam with a metal spoon.

3. Ladle hot mixture into hot, sterilized half-pint canning jars, leaving a ¼-inch headspace. Wipe jar rims; adjust lids and screw bands.

4. Process filled jars in a boiling-water canner 10 minutes (start timing when water returns to boiling). Remove jars from canner; cool on wire racks. Let spread stand for up to 2 weeks before using. **Makes 8 half-pint jars.**

*NOTE: Bananas should be fully ripe but with few or no brown spots showing.

PER 1 TABLESPOON: 38 cal., 0 g fat, 0 mg chol., 0 mg sodium, 10 g carb., 9 g sugars, 0 g fiber, 0 g pro.

✴ TEST KITCHEN TIP When selecting passion fruits, for the correct ripeness, choose those that have wrinkled skin.

Mango-Coconut Lime Conserve

3   medium limes

5   medium mangoes
    (about 4 lb.)

7½ cups sugar

1   6-oz. pkg. (2 foil pouches)
    liquid fruit pectin

½   tsp. butter

⅔   cup raw chip coconut,
    toasted if desired

1. Remove 3 tablespoons zest and squeeze 2 tablespoons juice from limes. You should have 2 tablespoons juice. Seed, peel, and coarsely chop mangoes (see page 127). You should have about 4 cups chopped mangoes.

2. Place mangoes in a 6- to 8-quart heavy pot; crush lightly with a potato masher. Stir in lime zest, lime peel, and sugar. Bring to boiling over medium heat, stirring to dissolve sugar. Quickly stir in pectin and butter. Bring to a full rolling boil, stirring constantly. Boil hard 1 minute, stirring constantly. Remove from heat. Quickly skim off foam with a metal spoon. Stir in coconut.

3. Ladle hot conserve into hot, sterilized half-pint canning jars, leaving a ¼-inch headspace. Wipe jar rims; adjust lids and screw bands.

4. Process filled jars in a boiling-water canner 5 minutes (start timing when water returns to boiling). Remove jars from canner; cool on wire racks. **Makes 8 half-pint jars.**

PER 1 TABLESPOON: 53 cal., 0 g fat, 0 mg chol., 0 mg sodium, 13 g carb., 13 g sugars, 0 g fiber, 0 g pro.

✳ TEST KITCHEN TIP A microplane grater with a small shred works well for removing zest from limes. Only remove the green layer. The white pith is bitter and will give the conserve a harsh taste.

Mango-Scotch Bonnet Jam

5 medium mangoes (about 4 lb.)

2 Tbsp. lime juice

2 medium fresh Scotch Bonnet or habañero peppers, seeded and minced (see page 119)

7½ cups sugar

½ of a 6-oz. pkg. (1 foil pouch) liquid fruit pectin

1. Seed and peel mangoes (see page 127). Place mangoes in a bowl. Use a potato masher to crush mangoes into a smooth pulp. Measure 4 cups mango pulp.

2. In a 6- to 8-quart heavy pot combine mango pulp, lime juice, and chile peppers. Stir in sugar. Bring to boiling over medium heat, stirring to dissolve sugar. Quickly stir in pectin. Bring to a full rolling boil, stirring constantly. Boil hard 1 minute, stirring constantly. Remove from heat. Quickly skim off foam with a metal spoon.

3. Ladle hot jam into hot, sterilized half-pint canning jars, leaving a ¼-inch headspace. Wipe jar rims; adjust lids and screw bands.

4. Process filled jars in a boiling-water canner 10 minutes (start timing when water returns to boiling). Remove jars from canner; cool on wire racks. **Makes 9 half-pint jars.**

PER 1 TABLESPOON: 52 cal., 0 g fat, 0 mg chol., 0 mg sodium, 13 g carb., 13 g sugars, 0 g fiber, 0 g pro.

✱ SIMPLY SERVE Fruit and heat marry for an assertive golden glaze. Brush this jam over salmon, chicken quarters, or pork tenderloin the last few minutes of grilling.

PREP: 30 MINUTES   **COOK:** 1 HOUR   **PROCESS:** 10 MINUTES

This chutney contains the signature Indian spice blend garam masala. The many different versions most often contain a mixture of warming spices, such as black pepper, cardamom, cloves, chiles, and cinnamon. The spices are toasted to bring out their flavors, then ground into a ready-to-use seasoning.

Curried Pineapple-Mango Chutney

- 5 cups chopped fresh pineapple
- 4 cups chopped fresh mangoes
- 2 cups chopped red sweet peppers
- 2 cups sugar
- 1 cup water
- 1 cup white wine vinegar
- 2 Tbsp. minced fresh ginger
- 1 Tbsp. garam masala
- 1 tsp. curry powder
- 1 to 2 fresh serrano peppers, finely chopped (see page 119)

1. In a 5- to 6-quart nonreactive heavy pot combine all the ingredients except the serrano peppers. Bring to boiling over medium-high heat, stirring frequently. Reduce heat; simmer, uncovered, about 1 hour or until mixture thickens, stirring occasionally. Stir in serrano peppers.

2. Ladle hot chutney into hot, sterilized half-pint canning jars, leaving a ¼-inch headspace. Wipe jar rims; adjust lids and screw bands.

3. Process filled jars in a boiling-water canner 10 minutes (start timing when water returns to boiling). Remove jars from canner; cool on wire racks. **Makes 7 half-pint jars.**

PER 1 TABLESPOON: 24 cal., 0 g fat, 0 mg chol., 24 mg sodium, 6 g carb., 5 g sugars, 0 g fiber, 0 g pro.

* TEST KITCHEN TIP To prepare mangoes, slice vertically down the sides of the seed in the middle. Score the mango halves, making a series of crosshatch cuts through the flesh just to the peel. Gently press on the skin of each half so the mango cubes stand out prominently. Cut the cubes off the peel.

Spiced Pineapple-Orange Sauce

4½ cups finely chopped fresh pineapple (about one 3-lb. pineapple)

½ of a vanilla bean

2 medium oranges

1 1.75-oz. pkg. powdered fruit pectin or 6 Tbsp. classic powdered fruit pectin

1 tsp. ground ginger

½ tsp. ground cardamom

½ tsp. butter

5½ cups sugar

1. Place pineapple in a 6- to 8-quart stockpot. Use a small sharp knife to scrape seeds from vanilla bean half (see page 218); add seeds to pot.

2. Using a vegetable peeler, remove the outer peel of the oranges in strips, being careful not to pick up the bitter white pith. Chop the orange peel and add to pot (reserve oranges for another use). Stir in the next four ingredients (through butter). Bring to a full rolling boil, stirring constantly. Quickly stir in sugar. Return to a full rolling boil, stirring constantly. Boil hard 1 minute, stirring constantly. Remove from heat. Quickly skim off foam with a metal spoon.

3. Ladle hot mixture into hot, sterilized half-pint canning jars, leaving a ¼-inch headspace. Wipe jar rims; adjust lids and screw bands.

4. Process filled jars in a boiling-water canner 10 minutes (start timing when water returns to boiling). Remove jars from canner; cool on wire racks. **Makes 7 half-pint jars.**

PER 1 TABLESPOON: 45 cal., 0 g fat, 0 mg chol., 0 mg sodium, 11 g carb., 11 g sugars, 0 g fiber, 0 g pro.

✳ TEST KITCHEN TIP You may wonder why some canning recipes call for a bit of butter. Butter helps reduce the foaming when making jams and jellies. Just a little makes a big difference.

Green-flesh kiwifruit is the most common. Gold kiwi, which is less hairy, has bright gold flesh and a flavor reminiscent of honey.

Lime-Kiwi Freezer Jam

2 limes

2 cups mashed, peeled kiwifruits (8 or 9 kiwifruits)

4 cups sugar

½ cup water

1 1.75-oz. pkg. regular powdered fruit pectin or 6 Tbsp. classic powdered fruit pectin

1. Remove 1 teaspoon zest and squeeze ¼ cup juice from limes. In a bowl combine lime zest, mashed kiwifruits, and sugar. Let stand 10 minutes, stirring occasionally. Meanwhile, in a small saucepan combine the water and lime juice. Stir in pectin. Bring to boiling. Boil hard 1 minute, stirring constantly. Add pectin mixture to the fruit mixture, stirring until sugar dissolves and mixture is not grainy. Cool 15 minutes.

2. Ladle jam into clean half-pint freezer containers, leaving a ½-inch headspace. Seal and label. Let stand at room temperature 24 hours before serving. Store up to 3 weeks in the refrigerator or up to 1 year in the freezer. **Makes 5 half-pint containers.**

PER 1 TABLESPOON: 46 cal., 0 g fat, 0 mg chol., 1 mg sodium, 12 g carb., 11 g sugars, 0 g fiber, 0 g pro.

Garden Favorites

Confetti Preserves

2 cups finely shredded carrots

2 cups finely shredded zucchini

2 cups finely shredded yellow summer squash

2 Tbsp. lemon juice

4½ cups sugar

1 tsp. apple pie spice

1 1.75-oz. pkg. powdered fruit pectin for lower-sugar recipes or 3 Tbsp. powdered fruit pectin for low- or no-sugar recipes

1. In a 6- to 8-quart heavy pot combine the first four ingredients (through lemon juice). In a bowl stir together ¼ cup of the sugar, the apple pie spice, and the pectin; stir into carrot mixture. Bring to a full rolling boil, stirring constantly. Stir in the remaining 4¼ cups sugar. Return to a full rolling boil, stirring constantly. Boil hard 1 minute, stirring constantly. Remove from heat. Quickly skim off any foam with a metal spoon.

2. Ladle hot preserves into hot, sterilized half-pint canning jars, leaving a ¼-inch headspace. Wipe jar rims; adjust lids and screw bands.

3. Process filled jars in a boiling-water canner 10 minutes (start timing when water returns to boiling). Remove jars from canner; cool on wire racks. **Makes 6 half-pint jars.**

PER 1 TABLESPOON: 46 cal., 0 g fat, 0 mg chol., 3 mg sodium, 12 g carb., 12 g sugars, 0 g fiber, 0 g pro.

★ TEST KITCHEN TIP Save time by cleaning all of the vegetables first, then give them a whirl in a food processor fitted with a fine-shredding blade.

Succotash is a savory dish of corn, peppers, zucchini, and lima beans. This chunky jam, a riff on the Southern classic, is a wonderful topper for grilled pork chops or flank steaks.

Succotash Jam

1½ cups finely chopped red sweet peppers

1½ cups fresh or frozen whole kernel corn

6½ cups sugar

1½ cups cider vinegar

½ cup chopped zucchini

¼ cup finely chopped red onion

½ tsp. crushed red pepper

1 6-oz. pkg. (2 foil pouches) liquid fruit pectin

1. Preheat broiler. Line a 15×10-inch baking pan with foil. Spread sweet pepper and corn in the prepared pan. Broil 3 to 4 inches from the heat 3 to 5 minutes or until tender and lightly charred, stirring once.

2. In a 6- to 8-quart heavy pot combine sweet pepper, corn, and the next five ingredients (through crushed red pepper). Bring to boiling, stirring constantly. Quickly stir in pectin. Bring to a full rolling boil, stirring constantly. Boil hard 1 minute, stirring constantly. Remove from heat. Quickly skim off foam with a metal spoon.

3. Ladle hot jam into hot, sterilized half-pint canning jars, leaving a ¼-inch headspace. Wipe jar rims; adjust lids and screw bands.

4. Process in a boiling-water canner 10 minutes (start timing when water returns to boiling). Remove jars; cool on wire racks. **Makes 7 half-pint jars.**

PER 1 TABLESPOON: 53 cal., 0 g fat, 0 mg chol., 1 mg sodium, 13 g carb., 13 g sugars, 0 g fiber, 0 g pro.

Poblano-Jalapeño Jelly

5½   cups sugar

2½   cups seeded and finely chopped fresh poblano chile peppers (about 4 peppers) (see page 119)

1   cup cider vinegar

½   cup water

½   cup seeded and finely chopped fresh jalapeño chile peppers* (3 to 4 peppers)

1½   tsp. salt

½   cup lime juice

1   6-oz. pkg. (2 foil pouches) liquid fruit pectin

Green food coloring (optional)

1. In a 6- to 8-quart heavy pot combine the first six ingredients (through salt). Bring to boiling. Cook 5 minutes, stirring frequently. Remove from heat. Cover and let stand 30 minutes.

2. Stir lime juice into pepper mixture. Bring to a full rolling boil, stirring constantly. Boil hard 1 minute, stirring constantly. Quickly stir in pectin. Return to a full rolling boil, stirring constantly. Boil hard 1 minute, stirring constantly. If desired, add a few drops of green food coloring to tint to desired color. Remove from heat.

3. Ladle hot jelly into hot, sterilized half-pint canning jars, leaving a ¼-inch headspace. Wipe rims; adjust lids and screw bands.

4. Process filled jars in a boiling-water canner 10 minutes (start timing when water returns to boiling). Remove jars from canner; cool on wire racks. **Makes 7 half-pint jars.**

PER 1 TABLESPOON: 41 cal., 0 g fat, 0 mg chol., 32 mg sodium, 10 g carb., 10 g sugars, 0 g fiber, 0 g pro.

* TEST KITCHEN TIP This jelly uses enough chopped chile peppers to justify pulling out the food processor to chop them. It's a good way to avoid contact with the spicy chiles.

Any kind of tomato is acceptable for this recipe. However, roma tomatoes have thick, dense flesh and low water content that make them the best choice for thick sauces and jams. Garden-fresh tomatoes will produce the best full-flavor jam.

Tandoori Tomato Jam

5 lb. ripe tomatoes, cored and finely chopped

3 cups sugar

½ cup bottled lime juice

2 tsp. salt

2 tsp. grated fresh ginger

1 tsp. crushed red pepper

2 tsp. garam masala

1. In a 4- to 6-quart nonreactive heavy pot combine the first six ingredients (through crushed red pepper). Bring to boiling; reduce heat. Simmer, uncovered, 1 hour 30 minutes to 1 hour 40 minutes or until reduced to a jamlike consistency and no excess liquid remains, stirring occasionally. Stir in garam masala.

2. Ladle hot jam into hot, sterilized half-pint canning jars, leaving a ¼-inch headspace. Wipe jar rims; adjust lids and screw bands.

3. Process filled jars in a boiling-water canner 10 minutes (start timing when water returns to boiling). Remove jars from canner; cool on wire racks. **Makes 5 half-pint jars.**

PER 1 TABLESPOON: 39 cal., 0 g fat, 0 mg chol., 92 mg sodium, 10 g carb., 9 g sugars, 0 g fiber, 0 g pro.

✱ TEST KITCHEN TIP To give the jam wonderful texture, do not peel or seed the tomatoes. For ease of preparation, cut the tomatoes into 1½-inch pieces and pulse in a food processor, one-fourth at a time, until finely chopped.

Rosemary Tomato Jam

5 lb. ripe tomatoes, cored and finely chopped (9½ cups)

3 cups sugar

½ cup white balsamic vinegar

2 Tbsp. finely chopped fresh rosemary

1 tsp. salt

1. In a 4- to 6-quart nonreactive heavy pot combine all ingredients. Bring to boiling; reduce heat. Simmer, uncovered, 2 hours 45 minutes to 3 hours or until reduced to a jamlike consistency and no excess liquid remains, stirring occasionally.

2. Ladle hot jam into hot, sterilized half-pint canning jars, leaving a ¼-inch headspace. Wipe jar rims; adjust lids and screw bands.

3. Process filled jars in a boiling-water canner 10 minutes (start timing when water returns to boiling). Remove jars from canner; cool on wire racks. **Makes 4 half-pint jars.**

PER 1 TABLESPOON: 46 cal., 0 g fat, 0 mg chol., 38 mg sodium, 12 g carb., 11 g sugars, 0 g fiber, 0 g pro.

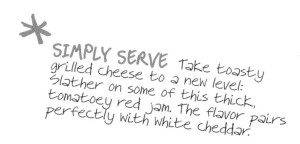

* SIMPLY SERVE Take toasty grilled cheese to a new level: slather on some of this thick, tomatoey red jam. The flavor pairs perfectly with white cheddar.

Honeydew is a very sweet melon; the addition of lime juice and lemon juice balances its sweetness with a bit of puckery acidity.

Lemon-Lime Honeydew Jelly

8   cups cubed honeydew melon

½   cup lime juice

½   cup lemon juice

1   1.75-oz. pkg. regular powdered fruit pectin or 6 Tbsp. classic powdered fruit pectin

4½   cups sugar

1. Place melon in a food processor, one-third at a time, and process until smooth. Pour pureed melon into a fine-mesh sieve set over a bowl. Press liquid from pulp; discard pulp. Measure 2 cups liquid.

2. In a 6- to 8-quart heavy pot combine the melon liquid, lime juice, lemon juice, and pectin. Bring to a full rolling boil over high heat, stirring constantly. Stir in sugar. Return to a full rolling boil, stirring constantly. Boil hard 1 minute, stirring constantly. Remove from heat. Quickly skim off foam with a metal spoon.

3. Ladle hot jelly into hot, sterilized half-pint canning jars, leaving a ¼-inch headspace. Wipe jar rims; adjust lids and screw bands.

4. Process filled jars in a boiling-water canner 5 minutes (start timing when water returns to boiling). Remove jars from canner; cool on wire racks. **Makes 5 half-pint jars.**

PER 1 TABLESPOON: 58 cal., 0 g fat, 0 mg chol., 2 mg sodium, 15 g carb., 14 g sugars, 0 g fiber, 0 g pro.

✱ SIMPLY SERVE Make a memorable cocktail: Use a couple spoonfuls of this unassuming jelly in place of simple syrup when mixing citrus-base drinks.

Choose regular green or golden-hue honeydew melon, depending on the color you want for this jam. Their flavors are similarly sweet.

Cucumber-Honeydew Jam

1 2¼-lb. golden honeydew or regular honeydew melon

1 cup shredded peeled and seeded cucumber

⅔ cup lime juice

6 cups sugar

½ tsp. butter

½ of a 6-oz. pkg. (1 foil pouch) liquid fruit pectin

1. Seed, peel, and cut melon into cubes (you should have 6 cups). Place cubed melon in a food processor, half at a time, and process until smooth. Pour pureed melon into a fine-mesh sieve set over a bowl. Allow liquid to drain from the pureed melon about 10 minutes, gently stirring occasionally. You should have 2½ cups pureed melon. Discard liquid in bowl.

2. In a 6- to 8-quart heavy pot combine the pureed melon and the next four ingredients (through butter). Bring to boiling, stirring constantly to dissolve sugar. Quickly stir in pectin. Bring to a full rolling boil, stirring constantly. Boil hard 1 minute, stirring constantly. Remove from heat. Quickly skim off foam with a metal spoon.

3. Ladle hot jam into hot, sterilized half-pint canning jars, leaving a ¼-inch headspace. Wipe jar rims; adjust lids and screw bands.

4. Process filled jars in a boiling-water canner 10 minutes (start timing when water returns to boiling). Remove jars from canner; cool on wire racks. **Makes 7 half-pint jars.**

PER 1 TABLESPOON: 51 cal., 0 g fat, 0 mg chol., 2 mg sodium, 13 g carb., 13 g sugars, 0 g fiber, 0 g pro.

A spoonful of this jewel-tone jelly will remind you of a favorite childhood hard candy. Steal a spoonful to savor all by itself!

Watermelon-Raspberry Jelly

3½ cups fresh raspberries

¼ cup water

4 cups chopped fresh watermelon

¼ cup lemon juice

7½ cups sugar

1 6-oz. pkg. (2 foil pouches) liquid fruit pectin

1. In a 6- to 8-quart heavy pot combine raspberries and the water. Bring to boiling; reduce heat. Simmer, covered, 5 minutes. Cool slightly. Transfer mixture to a blender or food processor. Cover and blend or process until pureed. Pour pureed berries into a fine-mesh sieve set over a large bowl; stir and press on fruit with a large spoon to remove juice. Discard seeds and pulp. You should have about 1⅓ cups juice.

2. In a blender or food processor combine watermelon and lemon juice. Cover and blend or process until smooth. Pour mixture into a fine-mesh sieve set over a large bowl; stir and press on fruit with a large spoon to remove juice. Discard pulp. You should have about 2⅓ cups juice. Combine the watermelon juice and raspberry juice; measure and add enough water to equal 4 cups.

3. In the same pot stir together juice mixture and sugar. Bring to boiling, stirring to dissolve sugar. Quickly stir in pectin. Bring to a full rolling boil, stirring constantly. Boil hard 1 minute, stirring constantly. Remove from heat. Quickly skim off foam with a metal spoon.

4. Ladle hot jelly into hot, sterilized half-pint canning jars, leaving a ¼-inch headspace. Wipe jar rims; adjust lids.

5. Process filled jars in a boiling-water canner 5 minutes (start timing when water returns to boiling). Remove jars from canner; cool on wire racks. **Makes 8 half-pint jars.**

PER 1 TABLESPOON: 49 cal., 0 g fat, 0 mg chol., 0 mg sodium, 13 g carb., 12 g sugars, 0 g fiber, 0 g pro.

* TEST KITCHEN TIP The amount of juice you get from your watermelon and raspberries may vary. The key is to only use 4 cups of liquid. If you have excess juice, discard the extra or save for another use. If you don't have enough juice, add water to make 4 cups.

Rhubarb-Raspberry Cinnamon Jam

4 cups crushed fresh
raspberries (about 2 lb.)

12 to 14 oz. fresh rhubarb,
chopped (3 cups)

¼ cup lemon juice

6 inches stick cinnamon

1 1.75-oz. pkg. regular
powdered fruit pectin or
6 Tbsp. classic powdered
fruit pectin

6 cups sugar

1. In a 6- to 8-quart heavy pot stir together the first four ingredients (through cinnamon). Stir in pectin. Bring to a full rolling boil, stirring constantly. Quickly stir in sugar. Return to a full rolling boil, stirring constantly. Boil hard 1 minute, stirring constantly. Remove from heat. Quickly skim off foam with a metal spoon. Remove and discard cinnamon.

2. Ladle hot jam into hot, sterilized half-pint canning jars, leaving a ¼-inch headspace. Wipe jar rims; adjust lids and screw bands.

3. Process filled jars in a boiling-water canner 10 minutes (start timing when water returns to boiling). Remove jars from canner; cool on wire racks. **Makes 8 half-pint jars.**

PER 1 TABLESPOON: 41 cal., 0 g fat, 0 mg chol., 0 mg sodium, 10 g carb., 10 g sugars, 0 g fiber, 0 g pro.

* TEST KITCHEN TIP Stick cinnamon adds a hint of warmth to this double-fruit jam. Use tongs or a slotted spoon to remove the cinnamon from the hot mixture.

Fresh red rhubarb is essential for making this pretty pink jam. Make it when gardens are bursting with this springtime favorite.

Spiced Orange-Rhubarb Jam

2½ lb. fresh rhubarb, trimmed and finely chopped (about 8 cups)

1 cup orange juice

1 1.75-oz. pkg. regular powdered fruit pectin or 6 Tbsp. classic powdered fruit pectin

1 tsp. ground cinnamon

½ tsp. ground ginger

¼ tsp. ground nutmeg

6½ cups sugar

1. In a 6- to 8-quart heavy pot combine rhubarb and orange juice. Bring to boiling; reduce heat. Simmer, uncovered, 2 minutes. Stir in the next four ingredients (through nutmeg). Bring to a full rolling boil, stirring constantly. Quickly stir in sugar. Return to a full rolling boil, stirring constantly. Boil hard 1 minute, stirring constantly. Remove from heat. Quickly skim off foam with a metal spoon.

2. Ladle hot jam into hot, sterilized half-pint canning jars, leaving a ¼-inch headspace. Wipe jar rims; adjust lids and screw bands.

3. Process filled jars in a boiling-water canner 10 minutes (start timing when water returns to boiling). Remove jars from canner; cool on wire racks. **Makes 8 half-pint jars.**

PER 1 TABLESPOON: 45 cal., 0 g fat, 0 mg chol., 0 mg sodium, 11 g carb., 11 g sugars, 0 g fiber, 0 g pro.

Hot Thai Sweet Potato-Pumpkin Butter

1½ to 2 lb. sweet potatoes

3 small fresh red Thai chile peppers (see page 119)

1 15-oz. can pumpkin

1 cup packed brown sugar

1 cup canned unsweetened coconut milk

2 Tbsp. lime juice

1 tsp. ground ginger

½ tsp. ground cinnamon

¼ tsp. salt

1. Preheat oven to 375°F. Place sweet potatoes in a 15×10-inch baking pan; prick each several times with a fork. Roast 60 to 70 minutes or until very tender. Add Thai peppers to the baking pan the last 6 minutes of roasting time; roast until tender and lightly browned in spots. Let sweet potatoes cool. Cut each sweet potato in half lengthwise. Scoop out pulp, discarding skins. Remove stems from peppers. Place sweet potato pulp and peppers in a food processor. Cover and process until very smooth. Measure 1¾ cups puree (save any remaining puree for another use).

2. In a 5-quart heavy pot combine sweet potato puree and remaining ingredients. Bring to boiling; reduce heat. Simmer, uncovered, about 20 minutes or until thickened and mixture mounds on a spoon, stirring frequently. (If mixture spatters, reduce heat.)

3. Place pot of sweet potato-pumpkin butter in a sink filled with ice water; stir to cool. Ladle into clean, wide-mouth half-pint freezer containers, leaving a ½-inch headspace. Seal and label. Store in the refrigerator up to 2 weeks or freeze up to 6 months. **Makes 4 half-pint containers.**

PER 2 TABLESPOONS: 61 cal., 2 g fat (1 g sat. fat), 0 mg chol., 30 mg sodium, 12 g carb., 8 g sugars, 1 g fiber, 1 g pro.

SIMPLY SERVE Spread this spicy butter on fried wonton wrappers, then sprinkle with toasted coconut, pepitas, and fresh chile pepper slices.

Carrots give color, fennel contributes flavor and texture, and figs provide sweetness for this spicy condiment, which makes a terrific hostess gift.

Carrot Fennel-Fig Chutney

- 4 cups chopped carrots
- 3 cups chopped, cored fennel bulbs (2 medium)
- 2 cups water
- 1½ cups sugar
- 1 tsp. ground coriander
- ½ tsp. ground ginger
- ½ tsp. black pepper
- ¼ tsp. ground cardamom
- ¼ tsp. ground allspice
- ¼ tsp. crushed red pepper
- 1 cup apple cider vinegar
- ¾ cup dried Calimyrna figs, stemmed and chopped
- ½ cup honey

1. In a 4- to 6-quart heavy pot combine the first 10 ingredients (through crushed red pepper). Bring to boiling, stirring to dissolve sugar; reduce heat. Simmer, covered, 10 to 12 minutes or until vegetables are tender. Use a potato masher to mash mixture slightly.

2. Add vinegar, figs, and honey. Return to boiling; reduce heat. Simmer, uncovered, about 30 minutes or until syrup is thickened, stirring frequently to prevent mixture from sticking to the bottom of the pan and burning. Remove from heat.

3. Ladle hot chutney into hot, sterilized half-pint canning jars, leaving a ½-inch headspace. Wipe jar rims; adjust lids and screw bands.

4. Process filled jars in a boiling-water canner 10 minutes (start timing when water returns to boiling). Remove jars from canner; cool on wire racks. **Makes 5 half-pint jars.**

PER 1 TABLESPOON: 35 cal., 0 g fat, 0 mg chol., 8 mg sodium, 9 g carb., 8 g sugars, 1 g fiber, 0 g pro.

✳ TEST KITCHEN TIP Fresh fennel bulbs have a light green hue and deep green feathery fronds on top. Look for crisp, clean bulbs without blemishes. Cut the bulbs into quarters from top to bottom, then cut out the tough core.

Our Best Blends

Cranberry Christmas Jam

1 cup fresh raspberries

4 cups finely chopped peeled, cored apples (about 1¼ lb.)

5 cups sugar

½ cup dried cranberries

¼ cup cranberry juice*

2 Tbsp. lemon juice

½ of a 6-oz. pkg. (1 pouch) liquid fruit pectin

1. Place raspberries in a 6- to 8-quart heavy pot; crush slightly. Stir in the next five ingredients (through lemon juice). Bring to a full rolling boil, stirring constantly. Quickly stir in pectin. Return to a full rolling boil, stirring constantly. Boil hard 1 minute, stirring constantly. Remove from heat. Quickly skim off foam with a metal spoon.

2. Ladle hot jam into hot, sterilized half-pint canning jars, leaving a ¼-inch headspace. Wipe jar rims; adjust lids and screw bands.

3. Process filled jars in a boiling-water canner 10 minutes (start timing when water returns to boiling). Remove jars from canner; cool on wire racks. **Makes 6 half-pint jars.**

PER 1 TABLESPOON: 46 cal., 0 g fat, 0 mg chol., 0 mg sodium, 12 g carb., 12 g sugars, 0 g fiber, 0 g pro.

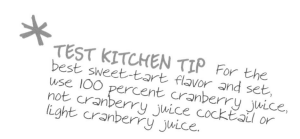

*TEST KITCHEN TIP For the best sweet-tart flavor and set, use 100 percent cranberry juice, not cranberry juice cocktail or light cranberry juice.

Pomegranate Cherry-Berry Compote

2 cups pitted fresh dark
   sweet cherries

1 cup fresh raspberries

1 cup fresh blueberries

3 cups sugar

1 cup pomegranate juice

1. In a 4-quart heavy pot combine all ingredients. Bring to boiling, stirring until sugar dissolves; reduce heat. Simmer, uncovered, about 20 minutes or until mixture is thickened and reduced to 4 cups, stirring frequently.

2. Ladle hot compote into hot, sterilized half-pint canning jars, leaving a ¼-inch headspace. Wipe jar rims; adjust lids and screw bands.

3. Process filled jars in a boiling-water canner 15 minutes (start timing when water returns to boiling). Remove jars from canner; cool on wire racks. **Makes 4 half-pint jars.**

PER ¼ CUP: 176 cal., 0 g fat, 0 mg chol., 2 mg sodium, 45 g carb., 43 g sugars, 1 g fiber, 0 g pro.

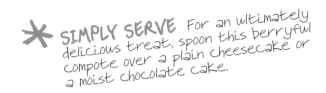

SIMPLY SERVE For an ultimately delicious treat, spoon this berryful compote over a plain cheesecake or a moist chocolate cake.

PREP: 30 MINUTES   COOK: 30 MINUTES   PROCESS: 10 MINUTES

Gooseberries are more likely to be found at farmers markets or you-pick berry farms than at supermarket. They are particularly high in pectin, which makes them a perfect addition to no-pectin-added jams.

Gooseberry-Mango Jam

6 cups fresh or frozen gooseberries

½ cup water

6 cups sugar

2 cups finely chopped, peeled mangoes (see page 127)

¼ cup lemon juice

1. Thaw gooseberries, if frozen. Remove and discard stems from gooseberries.

2. In a 6- to 8-quart heavy pot combine half of the gooseberries and the water. Use a potato masher to crush berries slightly. Stir in the remaining gooseberries and the remaining ingredients. Bring to boiling over medium heat, stirring constantly to dissolve sugar; reduce heat. Boil gently, uncovered, 30 to 40 minutes or until mixture sheets off a metal spoon and reaches 220°F (see page 78), stirring frequently (jam will be dark red in color). Remove from heat. Quickly skim off foam with a metal spoon.

3. Ladle hot jam into hot, sterilized half-pint canning jars, leaving a ¼-inch headspace. Wipe jar rims; adjust lids and screw bands.

4. Process filled jars in a boiling-water canner 10 minutes (start timing when water returns to boiling). Remove jars from canner; cool on wire racks. **Makes 6 half-pint jars.**

PER 1 TABLESPOON: 59 cal., 0 g fat, 0 mg chol., 0 mg sodium, 15 g carb., 15 g sugars, 0 g fiber, 0 g pro.

OUR BEST BLENDS **165**

Expect freezer jams to have a different consistency than boiling-water canner jams. They have a light, soft texture that spreads easily because it doesn't cling to the knife.

Strawberry-Mango Freezer Jam

1½ cups crushed fresh strawberries

½   cup crushed fresh mango pieces (see page 127)

1¼ cups sugar

3   Tbsp. powdered fruit pectin for low- or no-sugar recipes

½   cup orange juice

1. In a bowl stir together the crushed strawberries and mango.

2. In a medium saucepan stir together sugar and pectin until thoroughly mixed. Stir in orange juice. Bring mixture to boiling over medium-high heat, stirring constantly. Boil and stir 1 minute. Remove from heat. Quickly stir in the strawberry mixture until well combined.

3. Ladle jam into clean half-pint freezer containers, leaving a ½-inch headspace. Seal and label. Let stand at room temperature 24 hours before storing. Store in freezer up to 1 year or in refrigerator up to 3 weeks. **Makes 3 half-pint containers.**

PER 1 TABLESPOON: 24 cal., 0 g fat, 0 mg chol., 8 mg sodium, 6 g carb., 6 g sugars, 0 g fiber, 0 g pro.

Berry-Pepper Jelly

1½ cups cranberry-blueberry juice blend or other cranberry juice blend (not low-calorie)

1 cup vinegar

2 small fresh serrano chile peppers, halved (see page 119)

5 cups sugar

½ of a 6-oz. pkg. (1 foil pouch) liquid fruit pectin

1. In a medium heavy saucepan combine cranberry juice, vinegar, and chile peppers. Bring to boiling; reduce heat. Simmer, covered, 10 minutes. Strain mixture through a fine-mesh sieve set over a medium bowl; discard chile peppers. Measure 2 cups liquid.

2. In a 5- to 6-quart heavy pot combine the 2 cups liquid and the sugar. Bring to a full rolling boil, stirring constantly until sugar dissolves. Quickly stir in pectin. Return to a full rolling boil, stirring constantly. Boil hard 1 minute, stirring constantly. Remove from heat.

3. Ladle hot jelly into hot, sterilized half-pint canning jars, leaving a ¼-inch headspace. Wipe jar rims; adjust lids and screw bands.

4. Process filled jars in a boiling-water canner 5 minutes (start timing when water returns to boiling). Remove jars from canner; cool on wire racks. **Makes 5 half-pint jars.**

PER 1 TABLESPOON: 52 cal., 0 g fat, 0 mg chol., 1 mg sodium, 13 g carb., 13 g sugars, 0 g fiber, 0 g pro.

TEST KITCHEN TIP For a hotter jelly, stir in red or green serrano chile pepper slices (with or without seeds, which contain the most heat) with the pectin. Divide the pepper slices among the jars.

Dried Apricot-Fig Jam with Anise

16 oz. dried apricots, finely chopped

8 oz. dried figs, stemmed and finely chopped

5¾ cups water

3 lemons

3¼ cups sugar

1 1.75-oz. pkg. powdered fruit pectin for lower-sugar recipes or 3 Tbsp. powdered fruit pectin for low- or no-sugar recipes

1 tsp. orange zest

½ tsp. anise seeds, crushed

1. In a 4- to 6-quart heavy pot combine apricots and figs; add the water. Bring to boiling; remove from heat. Cover and let stand at least 1 hour or until fruit is fully plumped. Meanwhile, remove 1 teaspoon lemon zest and squeeze ½ cup juice from lemons.

2. Return fruit mixture to boiling, stirring frequently; reduce heat. Simmer, covered, 15 minutes, stirring occasionally. In a bowl combine ¼ cup of the sugar and the pectin. Stir pectin mixture, lemon zest, lemon juice, orange zest, and anise seeds into fruit mixture. Bring to a full rolling boil, stirring constantly. Stir in the remaining 3 cups sugar. Return to a full rolling boil, stirring constantly. Boil hard 1 minute, stirring constantly. Remove from heat. Quickly skim off foam with a metal spoon.

3. Ladle hot jam into hot, sterilized half-pint canning jars, leaving a ¼-inch headspace. Wipe jar rims; adjust lids and screw bands.

4. Process filled jars in a boiling-water canner 10 minutes (start timing when water returns to boiling). Remove jars from canner; cool on wire racks. **Makes 11 half-pint jars.**

PER 2 TABLESPOONS: 59 cal., 0 g fat, 0 mg chol., 2 mg sodium, 15 g carb., 14 g sugars, 1 g fiber, 0 g pro.

✳ SIMPLY SERVE smear this holiday-spiced jam on sandwich rolls and top with your choice of roasted meat and cheese. Pink-tinged pork tenderloin and Swiss or cheddar slices are good choices.

Vanilla bean paste is a specialty item. If you can't find it at your local market, check specialty kitchen stores or look online.

Blackberry-Plum Jam with Vanilla Bean

- 2 lb. fresh plums, pitted and finely chopped
- ½ cup water
- 7½ cups sugar
- 1¾ cups fresh blackberries, crushed (1 cup)
- ½ tsp. vanilla bean paste
- ½ of a 6-oz. pkg. (1 foil pouch) liquid fruit pectin

1. In a medium saucepan combine plums and the water. Bring to boiling; reduce heat. Simmer, covered, 5 minutes. Measure 3 cups mixture. In a 6- to 8-quart heavy pot combine plum mixture, sugar, crushed blackberries, and vanilla bean paste. Bring to boiling over medium heat, stirring constantly. Quickly stir in pectin. Bring to a full rolling boil, stirring constantly. Boil hard 1 minute, stirring constantly. Remove from heat. Quickly skim off foam with a metal spoon.

2. Ladle hot jam into hot, sterilized half-pint canning jars, leaving a ¼-inch headspace. Wipe jar rims; adjust lids and screw bands.

3. Process filled jars in a boiling-water canner 10 minutes (start timing when water returns to boiling). Remove jars from canner; cool on wire racks. **Makes 8 half-pint jars.**

PER 1 TABLESPOON: 57 cal., 0 g fat, 0 mg chol., 0 mg sodium, 15 g carb., 14 g sugars, 0 g fiber, 0 g pro.

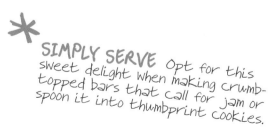

* SIMPLY SERVE Opt for this sweet delight when making crumb-topped bars that call for jam or spoon it into thumbprint cookies.

Two summertime fruits marry in a purple jam to create an unexpected and deliciously complex flavor combo.

Nectarine-Blueberry Jam

4 cups chopped ripe nectarines (about 2 lb.)

2 cups fresh blueberries

2 Tbsp. lemon juice

½ tsp. ground ginger

¼ tsp. ground nutmeg

6 cups sugar

½ cup pure maple syrup or honey

½ of a 6-oz. pkg. (1 foil pouch) liquid fruit pectin

1. In a 6- to 8-quart heavy pot combine the first five ingredients (through nutmeg). Using a potato masher, mash the fruit mixture to desired texture. Stir in sugar. Bring to boiling over medium heat, stirring constantly until sugar dissolves. Increase heat to medium-high; bring mixture to a full rolling boil, stirring constantly. Quickly stir in maple syrup and pectin. Return to a full rolling boil, stirring constantly. Boil hard 1 minute. Remove from heat. Quickly skim off foam with a metal spoon.

2. Ladle hot jam into hot, sterilized half-pint canning jars, leaving a ¼-inch headspace. Wipe jar rims; adjust lids and screw bands.

3. Process filled jars in a boiling-water canner 10 minutes (start timing when water returns to boiling). Remove jars from canner; cool on wire racks. **Makes 7 half-pint jars.**

PER 1 TABLESPOON: 49 cal., 0 g fat, 0 mg chol., 0 mg sodium, 13 g carb., 12 g sugars, 0 g fiber, 0 g pro.

Strawberry-Rhubarb Freezer Jam

3 cups fresh strawberries, hulled

1 cup finely chopped fresh rhubarb

5 cups sugar

½ tsp. lemon zest

¾ cup water

1 1.75-oz. pkg. regular powdered fruit pectin or 6 Tbsp. classic powdered fruit pectin

1. In a large bowl crush berries using a potato masher (you should have about 1½ cups). Stir rhubarb into the crushed berries. Stir in sugar and lemon zest. Let stand at room temperature 10 minutes, stirring occasionally.

2. In a small saucepan combine the water and pectin. Bring to boiling, stirring constantly. Boil hard 1 minute, stirring constantly. Remove from heat. Add pectin mixture to fruit mixture, stirring about 3 minutes or until sugar dissolves and mixture is no longer grainy.

3. Ladle jam into clean half-pint freezer containers, leaving a ½-inch headspace. Seal and label. Let stand at room temperature 24 hours before storing. Store in freezer up to 1 year or in refrigerator up to 3 weeks. **Makes 5 half-pint containers.**

PER 1 TABLESPOON: 53 cal., 0 g fat, 0 mg chol., 1 mg sodium, 14 g carb., 13 g sugars, 0 g fiber, 0 g pro.

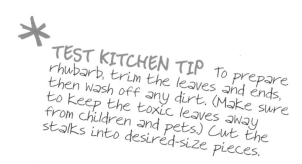

TEST KITCHEN TIP To prepare rhubarb, trim the leaves and ends, then wash off any dirt. (Make sure to keep the toxic leaves away from children and pets.) Cut the stalks into desired-size pieces.

Peach Melba is a classic combination of peach and raspberry. This jelly is a perfect filling for small doughnuts and layered cakes.

Peach Melba Jelly

3 cups fresh raspberries

2½ cups peach nectar

¼ cup bottled lemon juice

7½ cups sugar

1 6-oz. pkg. (2 foil pouches) liquid fruit pectin

1. Place raspberries in a blender. Cover and blend until smooth. Press pureed berries through a fine-mesh sieve; discard seeds. Measure 1 cup raspberry puree.

2. In an 8- to 10-quart heavy pot combine raspberry puree, peach nectar, and lemon juice. Stir in sugar. Bring to a full rolling boil, stirring to dissolve sugar. Quickly stir in pectin. Return to a full rolling boil, stirring constantly. Boil hard 1 minute, stirring constantly. Remove from heat. Quickly skim off foam with a metal spoon.

3. Ladle hot jelly into hot, sterilized half-pint canning jars, leaving a ¼-inch headspace. Wipe jar rims; adjust lids and screw bands.

4. Process filled jars in a boiling-water canner 5 minutes (start timing when water returns to boiling). Remove jars from canner; cool on wire racks. **Makes 10 half-pint jars.**

PER 1 TABLESPOON: 46 cal., 0 g fat, 0 mg chol., 0 mg sodium, 12 g carb., 11 g sugars, 0 g fiber, 0 g pro.

Spoon this jam onto pieces of hearty whole grain toast that have been spread with a little cream cheese. Your breakfast will taste like dessert.

Carrot Cake Jam

2 cups finely shredded carrots

1 cup finely chopped, peeled pear

1 15-oz. can crushed pineapple (juice pack), undrained

2 Tbsp. lemon juice

1 tsp. ground cinnamon

½ tsp. ground nutmeg

1 1.75-oz. pkg. regular powdered fruit pectin or 6 Tbsp. classic powdered fruit pectin

4 cups granulated sugar

2 cups packed brown sugar

¼ cup flaked coconut or raisins (optional)

1 tsp. vanilla

1. In a 4- to 6-quart heavy pot combine the first six ingredients (through nutmeg). Bring to boiling, stirring constantly; reduce heat. Simmer, covered, 20 minutes, stirring frequently. Remove from heat. Sprinkle carrot mixture with pectin; stir until pectin dissolves.

2. Bring carrot mixture to boiling, stirring constantly. Add sugars. Return to a full rolling boil. Boil 1 minute, stirring constantly. Remove from heat. Quickly skim off foam with a metal spoon. Stir in coconut (if desired) and vanilla.

3. Ladle hot jam into hot, sterilized half-pint canning jars, leaving a ¼-inch headspace. Wipe jar rims; adjust lids and screw bands.

4. Process filled jars in a boiling-water canner 10 minutes (start timing when water returns to boiling). Remove jars from canner; cool on wire racks. **Makes 7 half-pint jars.**

PER 1 TABLESPOON: 48 cal., 0 g fat, 0 mg chol., 3 mg sodium, 13 g carb., 12 g sugars, 0 g fiber, 0 g pro.

TEST KITCHEN TIP Save yourself some work! Young, tender carrots seldom need peeling. Just give them a good scrub with a stiff brush.

Lower Sugar

Three ranch breakfast favorites-bacon, maple syrup, and coffee-come together in this robust spread perfect for slathering on flapjacks and biscuits.

Cowboy Bacon-Shallot Jam

1 lb. thick-sliced bacon, chopped

Canola oil

2 lb. sweet onions, coarsely chopped

8 oz. shallots (about 8 medium), sliced

½ tsp. salt

2 Tbsp. snipped fresh oregano

1 tsp. ground ancho chile pepper

1 cup pure maple syrup

1 Tbsp. instant coffee crystals

¼ cup balsamic vinegar

1. In an extra-large skillet cook bacon over medium heat about 10 minutes or until browned. Using a slotted spoon, transfer bacon to paper towels. Drain and reserve bacon drippings. Measure drippings in a glass measuring cup. Add canola oil to reach ½ cup. Add oil mixture to skillet with onions, shallots, and salt. Cook over medium heat about 5 minutes or until onions start to soften, stirring frequently. Reduce heat to medium-low. Stir in oregano and ancho chile pepper. Cook, covered, 10 to 12 minutes or until onions are very tender, stirring twice.

2. Increase heat to medium-high. Add bacon, maple syrup, and coffee crystals. Bring just to boiling. Reduce heat to medium. Cook, uncovered, 50 to 60 minutes or until most of the liquid has evaporated, stirring frequently. Remove from heat; stir in vinegar.

3. Ladle mixture into clean half-pint freezer containers, leaving a ¼-inch headspace. Cool 30 minutes. Seal and label. Store in the refrigerator up to 1 month or freeze up to 6 months. Serve cold, at room temperature, or warmed. **Makes 3 half-pint containers.**

PER 1 TABLESPOON: 74 cal., 5 g fat (1 g sat. fat), 6 mg chol., 89 mg sodium, 7 g carb., 5 g sugars, 0 g fiber, 1 g pro.

CHAPTER 8

Happy Hour Specials

The same rule applies as when cooking with wine: Choose a tequila or orange liqueur that you would normally drink in your favorite cocktails. The quality shows through in the flavor of the jam.

Strawberry Margarita Jam

6 cups fresh strawberries, hulled

3 to 4 limes

½ cup tequila

¼ cup triple sec

6 cups sugar

½ of a 6-oz. pkg. (1 foil pouch) liquid fruit pectin

1. Place 1 cup of the strawberries in an 8- to 10-quart heavy pot. Use a potato masher to crush berries. Continue adding strawberries and crushing until you have 3 cups crushed berries. Remove 1 teaspoon lime zest and squeeze ⅔ cup juice from limes.

2. Stir lime juice, tequila, and triple sec into crushed berries. Gradually stir in sugar. Bring to a full rolling boil, stirring constantly. Quickly stir in pectin and lime zest. Return to a full rolling boil. Boil hard for 1 minute, stirring constantly. Remove from heat. Quickly skim off foam with a metal spoon.

3. Ladle hot jam into hot, sterilized half-pint canning jars, leaving a ¼-inch headspace. Wipe jar rims; adjust lids and screw bands.

4. Process filled jars in a boiling-water canner 10 minutes (start timing when water returns to boiling). Remove jars from canner; cool on wire racks. **Makes 7 half-pint jars.**

PER 1 TABLESPOON: 47 cal., 0 g fat, 0 mg chol., 0 mg sodium, 11 g carb., 11 g sugars, 0 g fiber, 0 g pro.

Whiskey Sour Cocktail Jelly

3 limes

2 lemons

4¼ cups sugar

1½ cups water

¼ cup bourbon

½ of a 6-oz. pkg. (1 foil pouch) liquid fruit pectin

5 maraschino cherries with stems

5 fresh orange slices

1. Juice the limes and lemons (you will need 6 tablespoons of each). In a 6-quart heavy pot stir together lime juice and lemon juice, sugar, the water, and bourbon. Cook over high heat until mixture comes to a full rolling boil, stirring constantly. Quickly stir in pectin. Return to a full rolling boil; boil hard 1 minute, stirring constantly. Remove from heat. Quickly skim off foam with a metal spoon.

2. Place one cherry and one orange slice in each of five hot, sterilized half-pint canning jars. Ladle hot jelly into jars, leaving a ¼-inch headspace. Wipe jar rims; adjust lids and screw bands.

3. Process filled jars in a boiling-water canner 5 minutes (start timing when water returns to boiling). Remove jars from canner; cool on wire racks. Allow jars to stand at room temperature at least 1 week for jelly to set. **Makes 5 half-pint jars.**

PER 1 TABLESPOON: 45 cal., 0 g fat, 0 mg chol., 0 mg sodium, 11 g carb., 11 g sugars, 0 g fiber, 0 g pro.

✱ TEST KITCHEN TIP To keep fruit suspended, start with orange slices that are a bit larger than the diameter of the jar. Wedge one down in each jar, trapping the cherry underneath, so fruit stays near center of jar when jelly is added.

Bloody Mary Jam

5 lb. ripe tomatoes, cored and finely chopped* (9 cups)

3 cups sugar

½ cup finely chopped onion

½ cup bottled lemon juice

1 Tbsp. Worcestershire sauce

2 tsp. prepared horseradish

1 tsp. salt

¼ tsp. celery seeds

¼ tsp. hot pepper sauce

¼ tsp. black pepper

¼ cup vodka

1. In a 4- to 6-quart nonreactive heavy pot combine all ingredients, except vodka. Bring to boiling; reduce heat. Simmer, uncovered, about 3 hours or until no excess liquid remains and mixture is thick and mounds on a spoon, stirring occasionally. Stir in vodka.

2. Ladle hot jam into hot, sterilized half-pint canning jars, leaving a ¼-inch headspace. Wipe jar rims; adjust lids and screw bands.

3. Process filled jars in a boiling-water canner 10 minutes (start timing when water returns to boiling). Remove jars from canner; cool on wire racks. **Makes 4 half-pint jars.**

*NOTE: Do not peel or seed tomatoes. For easy prep, cut tomatoes into about 1¼-inch pieces and pulse in a food processor, one-fourth at time, until finely chopped.

PER 1 TABLESPOON: 46 cal., 0 g fat, 0 mg chol., 42 mg sodium, 11 g carb., 10 g sugars, 0 g fiber, 0 g pro.

*
SIMPLY SERVE substitute this tomatoey jam, which boasts all the flavors of the choice brunch beverage, for wing sauce when grilling or broiling chicken wings.

This deep red jelly with its rich wine flavor makes an impressive gift. Present it with a basket of assorted cheeses and crackers.

Sangria Jelly

2 oranges

2 limes

1 bottle dry red wine
   (3¼ cups)

5 cups sugar

1 6-oz. pkg. (2 foil pouches)
   liquid fruit pectin

2 Tbsp. brandy

1. Remove 2 teaspoons zest and squeeze ½ cup juice from oranges. Remove 1 teaspoon zest and ¼ cup juice from limes. In a 5- or 6-quart heavy pot combine the zests, juices, and wine. Stir in sugar. Bring to a full rolling boil, stirring constantly to dissolve sugar. Quickly stir in pectin. Bring to a full rolling boil, stirring constantly. Boil hard 1 minute, stirring constantly. Remove from heat. Quickly skim off foam with a metal spoon. Sir in brandy.

2. Ladle hot jelly into hot, sterilized half-pint canning jars, leaving a ¼-inch headspace. Wipe jar rims; adjust lids and screw bands.

3. Process filled jars in a boiling-water canner 5 minutes (start timing when water returns to boiling). Remove jars from canner; cool on wire racks. **Makes 8 half-pint jars.**

PER 1 TABLESPOON: 42 cal., 0 g fat, 0 mg chol., 0 mg sodium, 9 g carb., 9 g sugars, 0 g fiber, 0 g pro.

Champagne Pomegranate Jelly

1½ cups champagne or sparkling white wine

1¼ cups pomegranate juice

¼ cup lemon juice

1 1.75-oz. pkg. regular powdered fruit pectin or 6 Tbsp. classic powdered fruit pectin

4½ cups sugar

½ tsp. butter

1. In a 6-quart heavy pot combine the first four ingredients (through pectin). Bring mixture to a full rolling boil, stirring constantly. Stir in sugar and butter. Return to a full rolling boil, stirring constantly. Boil hard 1 minute, stirring constantly. Remove from heat. Quickly skim off foam with a metal spoon.

2. Ladle hot jelly into hot, sterilized half-pint canning jars, leaving a ¼-inch headspace. Wipe jar rims; adjust lids and screw bands.

3. Process filled jars in a boiling-water canner 5 minutes (start timing when water returns to boiling). Remove jars from canner; cool on wire racks. **Makes 5 half-pint jars.**

PER 1 TABLESPOON: 54 cal., 0 g fat, 0 mg chol., 1 mg sodium, 13 g carb., 13 g sugars, 0 g fiber, 0 g pro.

* SIMPLY SERVE Elevate a basic white cake to a spectacular holiday dessert. Sandwich this festive spread between cake layers, then sprinkle pomegranate seeds over the top of the frosted cake.

PREP: 35 MINUTES   PROCESS: 10 MINUTES

Blackberry-Port Jam

4 cups fresh blackberries

5½ cups sugar

1 1.75-oz. pkg. regular powdered fruit pectin or 6 Tbsp. classic powdered fruit pectin

1 cup vintage port

¼ tsp. ground cloves

1. Place the blackberries in an 8- to 10-quart heavy pot. Use a potato masher to crush the berries slightly. In a bowl combine ¼ cup of the sugar and the pectin; gradually stir into the berries. Stir in port and cloves.

2. Bring to a full rolling boil, stirring constantly. Add the remaining 5¼ cups sugar. Return to a full rolling boil, stirring constantly. Boil, uncovered, about 1 minute or until jam sheets off a metal spoon, stirring constantly. Remove from heat. Quickly skim off foam with a metal spoon.

3. Ladle hot jam into hot, sterilized half-pint canning jars, leaving a ¼-inch headspace. Wipe jar rims; adjust lids and screw bands.

4. Process filled jars in a boiling-water canner 10 minutes (start timing when water returns to boiling). Remove jars from canner; cool on wire racks until set. **Makes 8 half-pint jars.**

PER 1 TABLESPOON: 51 cal., 0 g fat, 0 mg chol., 0 mg sodium, 12 g carb., 12 g sugars, 0 g fiber, 0 g pro.

* TEST KITCHEN TIP Vintage port adds top quality to this special jam. Sip a glass of port as you enjoy a small plate with this jam, Stilton cheese, crackers, and almonds. Or slather it on fresh-baked biscuits for a holiday morning treat.

PREP: 45 MINUTES   **PROCESS:** 10 MINUTES

Peach Bellini Jam

7½ cups sugar

3 cups finely chopped, peeled ripe peaches (see page 11)

1 cup Prosecco or other sparkling white wine

2 Tbsp. lemon juice

½ of a 6-oz. pkg. (1 foil pouch) liquid fruit pectin

1. In a 6- to 8-quart nonreactive heavy pot combine the first four ingredients (through lemon juice). Bring to a full rolling boil, stirring constantly until sugar dissolves. Quickly stir in liquid pectin. Return to a full rolling boil, stirring constantly. Boil hard 1 minute, stirring constantly. Remove from heat. Quickly skim off foam with a metal spoon.

2. Ladle hot jam into hot, sterilized half-pint canning jars, leaving a ¼-inch headspace. Wipe jar rims; adjust lids and screw bands.

3. Process filled jars in a boiling-water canner 10 minutes (start timing when water returns to boiling). Remove jars from canner; cool on wire racks. **Makes 8 half-pint jars.**

PER 1 TABLESPOON: 49 cal., 0 g fat, 0 mg chol., 0 mg sodium, 12 g carb., 12 g sugars, 0 g fiber, 0 g pro.

* SIMPLY SERVE To make a Peach Bellini float, combine this magnificent jam with soda water and a couple scoops of vanilla ice cream.

When red or purple plums are at their summertime peak, make these holiday drink-inspired preserves to enjoy year-round.

Mulled Plum-Wine Preserves

3 lb. ripe plums, pitted and finely chopped (7 cups)

¾ cup dry red wine or orange juice

2 medium oranges, peeled, seeded, and sectioned

1 1.75-oz. pkg. regular powdered fruit pectin or 6 Tbsp. classic powdered fruit pectin

1 tsp. ground cinnamon

¼ tsp. ground allspice

⅛ tsp. ground cloves

8 cups sugar

1. In a 6- to 8-quart heavy pot combine plums and wine. Bring to boiling; reduce heat. Simmer, uncovered, 5 minutes. Stir in oranges. Measure 6 cups mixture; return to pot. Stir in the next four ingredients (through cloves). Bring to boiling, stirring constantly. Quickly stir in sugar. Bring to a full rolling boil, stirring constantly. Boil hard 1 minute, stirring constantly. Remove from heat. Quickly skim off foam with a metal spoon.

2. Ladle hot preserves into hot, sterilized half-pint canning jars, leaving a ¼-inch headspace. Wipe jar rims; adjust lids and screw bands.

3. Process filled jars in a boiling-water canner 10 minutes (start timing when water returns to boiling). Remove jars from canner; cool on wire racks. **Makes 10 half-pint jars.**

PER 1 TABLESPOON: 47 cal., 0 g fat, 0 mg chol., 0 mg sodium, 12 g carb., 11 g sugars, 0 g fiber, 0 g pro.

This marmalade won't turn you into a zombie! The alcohol content typical of the popular cocktail is greatly reduced, but it helps maintain fabulous fruit flavor and color.

Zombie Marmalade

- 2 large pink grapefruits
- 1 orange
- 1 medium lime
- 1⅓ cups water
- ⅛ tsp. baking soda
- 2 2-inch sticks cinnamon, broken
- 1 tsp. whole cloves
- 5 cups sugar
- ½ of a 6-oz. pkg. (1 foil pouch) liquid fruit pectin
- 2 Tbsp. dark rum
- 1 Tbsp. grenadine syrup

1. Score the peel of each grapefruit, the orange, and the lime into four lengthwise sections; remove peels with your fingers*. Use a sharp knife to scrape off the white portions of peels. Cut peels into thin strips and coarsely chop. In a medium saucepan combine peels, the water, and baking soda. Bring to boiling; reduce heat. Simmer, covered, 20 minutes. Do not drain.

2. Meanwhile, section citrus fruits (see page 103), reserving juices. Add fruit and juices to peel mixture; return to boiling. Simmer, covered, 10 minutes (you should have about 3 cups fruit mixture).

3. Place cinnamon and cloves in the center of a double-thick piece of 100-percent-cotton cheesecloth. Gather the cloth and tie with 100-percent-cotton kitchen string. In a 6- to 8-quart heavy pot combine spice bag, fruit mixture, and the sugar. Bring to a full rolling boil, stirring constantly. Quickly stir in pectin. Return to a full rolling boil; boil 1 minute, stirring constantly. Remove from heat. Remove spice bag. Skim off foam with a metal spoon. Stir in rum and grenadine syrup.

4. Ladle hot marmalade into hot, sterilized half-pint canning jars, leaving a ¼-inch headspace. Wipe jar rims; adjust lids and screw bands.

5. Process filled jars in a boiling-water canner 5 minutes (start timing when water returns to boiling). Remove jars; cool on wire racks. Let marmalade stand 2 weeks before serving.

Makes 5 half-pint jars.

*NOTE: Use a sharp vegetable peeler to remove peel from fruit in large strips. Remove any pith left on the peel as directed.

PER 1 TABLESPOON: 53 cal., 0 g fat, 0 mg chol., 2 mg sodium, 13 g carb., 13 g sugars, 0 g fiber, 0 g pro.

Go south of the border with this golden tequila-spiked jam that's laced with the warmth of ground ancho chile. Add some sweet heat to chicken quesadillas by spooning some over the tops.

Spicy Nectarine Smash Jam

- 4½ cups finely chopped ripe nectarines (2 lb.)
- 2 Tbsp. tequila or orange juice
- 2 tsp. ground ancho chile pepper
- 1 1.75-oz. pkg. regular powdered fruit pectin or 6 Tbsp. classic powdered fruit pectin
- 6 cups sugar

1. In a 6- to 8-quart heavy pot stir together nectarines, tequila, and ancho pepper. Stir in pectin. Bring to a full rolling boil, stirring constantly. Quickly stir in sugar. Return to a full rolling boil, stirring constantly. Boil hard 1 minute, stirring constantly. Remove from heat. Quickly skim off foam with a metal spoon.

2. Ladle hot jam into hot, sterilized half-pint canning jars, leaving a ¼-inch headspace. Wipe jar rims; adjust lids and screw bands.

3. Process filled jars in a boiling-water canner 10 minutes (start timing when water returns to boiling). Remove jars from canner; cool on wire racks. **Makes 6 half-pint jars.**

PER 1 TABLESPOON: 48 cal., 0 g fat, 0 mg chol., 0 mg sodium, 12 g carb., 12 g sugars, 0 g fiber, 0 g pro.

CHAPTER 9

Simply Syrups & Sauces

Blood oranges are slightly more tart than naval oranges, making this burnt orange-color syrup a more adult offering. Drizzle it over blueberry-studded pancakes and waffles.

Blood Orange Syrup

6 lb. blood oranges

2 cups water

3 cups sugar

1. Peel and section oranges (you should have about 11 cups). Place half of the orange sections in a 6- to 8-quart pot. Use a potato masher to crush oranges. Add the remaining orange sections and crush again. Add the water. Bring to boiling; reduce heat. Simmer, uncovered, 5 minutes, stirring occasionally.

2. Line a colander with a double layer of 100-percent-cotton cheesecloth; place over a large bowl. Pour crushed oranges into colander. Let stand to allow juice to drain. When cool enough to handle, bring the cheesecloth up to enclose the oranges. Press on the cheesecloth to release the juice. Discard oranges remaining in cheesecloth.

3. In the same pot heat the juice to a full rolling boil; stir in sugar. Continue boiling, uncovered, at a moderate, steady rate 20 to 30 minutes or until mixture is slightly thickened (the consistency of warm maple syrup), stirring frequently to prevent sticking.

4. Pour hot syrup into hot, sterilized half-pint canning jars, leaving a ¼-inch headspace. Wipe jar rims; adjust lids and screw bands.

5. Process filled jars in a boiling-water canner 5 minutes (start timing when water returns to boiling). Remove jars from canner; cool on wire racks. **Makes 4 half-pint jars.**

PER 1 TABLESPOON: 51 cal., 0 g fat, 0 mg chol., 0 mg sodium, 13 g carb., 12 g sugars, 1 g fiber, 0 g pro.

Caramel Apple Syrup

3 lb. tart green apples, peeled, cored, and finely chopped (about 6½ cups)

4 cups water

2 cups packed brown sugar

1 cup granulated sugar

1. Place apples in a 6- to 8-quart pot. Add the water. Bring to boiling; reduce heat. Simmer, covered, 15 minutes, stirring occasionally.

2. Line a colander with a double layer of 100-percent-cotton cheesecloth; place over a large bowl. Pour apple mixture into colander. Let stand to allow juice to drain. When cool enough to handle, bring the cheesecloth up to enclose the apples. Press on the cheesecloth to release the juice. Discard apples remaining in cheesecloth.

3. In the same pot heat the juice to a full rolling boil; stir in both sugars. Continue boiling, uncovered, at a moderate, steady rate 20 minutes, stirring frequently to prevent sticking.

4. Pour hot syrup into hot, sterilized half-pint canning jars, leaving a ¼-inch headspace. Wipe jar rims; adjust lids and screw bands.

5. Process filled jars in a boiling-water canner 5 minutes (start timing when water returns to boiling). Remove jars from canner; cool on wire racks. **Makes 4 half-pint jars.**

PER 1 TABLESPOON: 54 cal., 0 g fat, 0 mg chol., 3 mg sodium, 14 g carb., 13 g sugars, 0 g fiber, 0 g pro.

✻ SIMPLY SERVE sauté thin apple slices in butter to top a plate of French toast, then finish with this caramely good syrup.

Strawberry-Chile Syrup

2   limes

3½   cups hulled fresh
     strawberries (3½ lb.)

1¾   cups water

1   1-inch piece fresh ginger,
     peeled and thinly sliced

3   cups sugar

½   tsp. crushed red pepper

1. Use a vegetable peeler or sharp knife to remove only the green portion of the lime peel. Reserve limes for another use.

2. Place half of the berries in a 6- to 8-quart heavy pot. Use a potato masher to crush berries. Add the remaining berries and crush again. Add the water, lime peel, and ginger pieces. Bring to boiling; reduce heat. Simmer, uncovered, 5 minutes, stirring occasionally. Remove from heat; let stand 15 minutes.

3. Line a colander with a double layer of 100-percent-cotton cheesecloth; place over a large bowl. Pour crushed berries into colander. Let stand to allow juice to drain. When cool enough to handle, bring the cheesecloth up to enclose the strawberry mixture. Press on the cheesecloth to release the juice. Discard strawberry mixture remaining in cheesecloth.

4. In the same pot heat the juice to a full rolling boil; stir in sugar and crushed red pepper. Continue boiling, uncovered, at a moderate, steady rate 20 to 30 minutes or until mixture is slightly thickened (the consistency of warm maple syrup) and reaches 220°F, stirring frequently to prevent sticking. Remove from heat. Skim off foam with a metal spoon.

5. Pour hot syrup into hot, sterilized half-pint canning jars, leaving a ¼-inch headspace. Wipe jar rims; adjust lids and screw bands.

6. Process filled jars in a boiling-water canner 5 minutes (start timing when water returns to boiling). Remove jars from canner; cool on wire racks. **Makes 3 half-pint jars.**

PER 1 TABLESPOON: 60 cal., 0 g fat, 0 mg chol., 1 mg sodium, 15 g carb., 14 g sugars, 1 g fiber, 0 g pro.

* TEST KITCHEN TIP Use a candy thermometer to monitor the temperature of the syrup. Clip the thermometer on the side of the pot, making sure the tip does not touch the bottom of the pot.

PREP: 20 MINUTES   COOK: 25 MINUTES   PROCESS: 5 MINUTES

Lemon-Blueberry Syrup

3 lemons

6 cups fresh blueberries

4 cups water

3 cups sugar

1. Remove 3 tablespoons zest and squeeze 2 tablespoons juice from the lemons. Place half of the berries in a 6- to 8-quart pot. Use a potato masher to crush berries. Add the remaining berries and crush again. Add the water, lemon zest, and lemon juice. Bring to boiling; reduce heat. Simmer, uncovered, 5 minutes, stirring occasionally.

2. Line a colander with a double layer of 100-percent-cotton cheesecloth; place over a large bowl. Pour berry mixture into colander. Let stand to allow juice to drain. When cool enough to handle, bring the cheesecloth up to enclose the berry mixture. Press on the cheesecloth to release the juice. Discard berry mixture remaining in cheesecloth.

3. In the same pot heat the juice to a full rolling boil; stir in sugar. Continue boiling, uncovered, at a moderate, steady rate about 20 minutes or until mixture is slightly thickened (the consistency of warm maple syrup), stirring frequently to prevent sticking.*

4. Pour hot syrup into hot, sterilized half-pint canning jars, leaving a ¼-inch headspace. Wipe jar rims; adjust lids and screw bands.

5. Process filled jars in a boiling-water canner 5 minutes (start timing when water returns to boiling). Remove jars from canner; cool on wire racks. **Makes 5 half-pint jars.**

*NOTE: Because the natural pectin in blueberries is so high, this syrup will become jellylike if it is cooked too long. Follow the recommended cooking times exactly.

PER 1 TABLESPOON: 36 cal., 0 g fat, 0 mg chol., 1 mg sodium, 9 g carb., 9 g sugars, 0 g fiber, 0 g pro.

*SIMPLY SERVE For a fruity vinaigrette, combine equal parts olive oil and white wine vinegar in a jar, then add a tablespoon or two of this syrup. Shake it up and use it to dress a salad of greens and mixed berries.

Spiced Raspberry Syrup

3½ lb. fresh raspberries

2 cups water

3 cups sugar

1½ tsp. ground cinnamon

½ tsp. grated whole nutmeg

¼ tsp. ground cloves

1. Place half of the berries in a 6- to 8-quart pot. Use a potato masher to crush berries. Add the remaining berries and crush again. Add the water. Bring to boiling; reduce heat. Simmer, uncovered, 5 minutes, stirring occasionally.

2. Line a colander with a double layer of 100-percent-cotton cheesecloth; place over a large bowl. Pour berry mixture into colander. Let stand to allow juice to drain. When cool enough to handle, bring the cheesecloth up to enclose the berry mixture. Press on the cheesecloth to release the juice. Discard berry mixture remaining in cheesecloth.

3. In the same pot heat the juice to a full rolling boil; stir in sugar and spices. Continue boiling, uncovered, at a moderate, steady rate 20 to 30 minutes or until mixture is slightly thickened (the consistency of warm maple syrup), stirring frequently to prevent sticking.

4. Pour hot syrup into hot, sterilized half-pint canning jars, leaving a ¼-inch headspace. Wipe jar rims; adjust lids and screw bands.

5. Process filled jars in a boiling-water canner 5 minutes (start timing when water returns to boiling). Remove jars from canner; cool on wire racks. **Makes 3 half-pint jars + about ⅔ cup.**

PER SERVING: 51 cal., 0 g fat, 0 mg chol., 1 mg sodium, 13 g carb., 12 g sugars, 1 g fiber, 0 g pro.

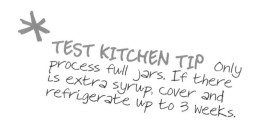

TEST KITCHEN TIP Only process full jars. If there is extra syrup, cover and refrigerate up to 3 weeks.

Vanilla-Peach Syrup

1   vanilla bean

12 cups sliced, peeled (see page 11) fresh peaches (3½ lb.)

2   cups water

2½ cups sugar

1. Cut the vanilla bean in half lengthwise. Scrape seeds from the pod; set seeds aside. Place half of the peaches in a 6- to 8-quart pot. Use a potato masher to crush peaches. Add the remaining peaches and crush again. Add the water and vanilla bean pod. Bring to boiling; reduce heat. Simmer, uncovered, 5 minutes, stirring occasionally.

2. Line a colander with a double layer of 100-percent-cotton cheesecloth; place over a large bowl. Pour peach mixture into colander. Let stand to allow juice to drain. When cool enough to handle, bring the cheesecloth up to enclose the peach mixture. Press on the cheesecloth to release the juice. Discard peach mixture remaining in cheesecloth.

3. In the same pot heat the juice to a full rolling boil; stir in the sugar and vanilla bean seeds. Continue boiling, uncovered, at a moderate, steady rate 20 to 30 minutes or until mixture is slightly thickened (the consistency of warm maple syrup) and reaches 220°F, stirring frequently to prevent sticking.

4. Pour hot syrup into hot, sterilized half-pint canning jars, leaving a ¼-inch headspace. Wipe jar rims; adjust lids and screw bands.

5. Process filled jars in a boiling-water canner 5 minutes (start timing when water returns to boiling). Remove jars from canner; cool on wire racks. **Makes 5 half-pint jars.**

PER 1 TABLESPOON: 51 cal., 0 g fat, 0 mg chol., 1 mg sodium, 13 g carb., 12 g sugars, 1 g fiber, 0 g pro.

★ TEST KITCHEN TIP Cut vanilla bean pods in half lengthwise. Place halves, cut sides up, on a cutting board, then use a paring knife to scrape the seeds out of the pod halves.

Black Forest Dessert Sauce

3 lb. ripe dark sweet cherries, pitted and chopped (7 cups)

1 1.75-oz. pkg. regular powdered fruit pectin or 6 Tbsp. classic powdered fruit pectin

2 Tbsp. orange juice

5 cups sugar

2 tsp. instant espresso coffee powder

2 Tbsp. kirsch or cherry brandy

2 oz. unsweetened chocolate, chopped

1. In a 6- to 8-quart heavy pot combine cherries, pectin, and orange juice. Bring to boiling, stirring constantly. Stir in sugar and espresso powder. Bring to a full rolling boil, stirring constantly. Boil hard 1 minute, stirring constantly. Remove from heat. Quickly skim off foam with a metal spoon. Stir in kirsch and chocolate.

2. Ladle hot sauce into hot, sterilized half-pint canning jars, leaving a ¼-inch headspace. Wipe jar rims; adjust lids and screw bands.

3. Process filled jars in a boiling-water canner 10 minutes (start timing when water returns to boiling). Remove jars from canner; cool on wire racks. **Makes 8 half-pint jars.**

PER 2 TABLESPOONS: 96 cal., 1 g fat (0 g sat. fat), 0 mg chol., 0 mg sodium, 22 g carb., 21 g sugars, 1 g fiber, 0 g pro.

* SIMPLY SERVE Spoon this deliciously decadent sauce over a scoop of vanilla bean ice cream on top of dark chocolate cake. Wunderbar!

Chai-Spiced Nectarine Sauce

6 cardamom pods

3 4-inch cinnamon sticks

5 cups sliced fresh
nectarines (about
6 medium)

2½ cups sugar

¼ cup water

1. Place cardamom pods and cinnamon sticks on a 6-inch square of double-thick 100-percent-cotton cheesecloth. Bring up the edges and tie closed with clean kitchen string to make a bag.

2. In a 6- to 8-quart pot combine the remaining ingredients. Add the spice bag. Bring to boiling, stirring to dissolve sugar; reduce heat. Simmer, uncovered, about 25 minutes or until sauce is thickened and reduced to about 3½ cups, stirring occasionally. Remove and discard spice bag.

3. Ladle hot sauce into hot, sterilized half-pint canning jars, leaving a ¼-inch headspace. Wipe jar rims; adjust lids and screw bands.

4. Process filled jars in a boiling-water canner 15 minutes (start timing when water returns to boiling). Remove jars from canner; cool on wire racks. **Makes 4 half-pint jars.**

PER ¼ CUP: 188 cal., 0 g fat, 0 mg chol., 1 mg sodium, 48 g carb., 46 g sugars, 1 g fiber, 1 g pro.

✳ SIMPLY SERVE Creamy rice pudding or vanilla ice cream makes a lovely, uncomplicated canvas for this coffee shop-inspired sauce.

PREP: 20 MINUTES   COOK: 25 MINUTES   PROCESS: 15 MINUTES

Chunky Pineapple Sauce

2 fresh pineapples, peeled, cored, and chopped (9 cups)

3 cups sugar

¼ cup water

3 Tbsp. chopped fresh basil

1. In a 6- to 8-quart heavy pot combine pineapple, sugar, and the water. Bring to boiling, stirring just until sugar dissolves; reduce heat. Simmer, uncovered, about 25 minutes or until sauce is thickened and reduced to about 6 cups, stirring occasionally. Stir in basil.

2. Ladle hot sauce into hot, sterilized half-pint canning jars, leaving a ¼-inch headspace. Wipe jar rims; adjust lids and screw bands.

3. Process filled jars in a boiling-water canner 15 minutes (start timing when water returns to boiling). Remove jars from canner; cool on wire racks. **Makes 6 half-pint jars.**

PER ¼ CUP: 171 cal., 0 g fat, 0 mg chol., 1 mg sodium, 44 g carb., 42 g sugars, 1 g fiber, 0 g pro.

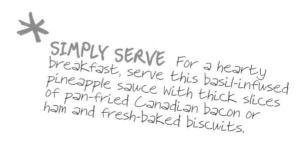

* SIMPLY SERVE For a hearty breakfast, serve this basil-infused pineapple sauce with thick slices of pan-fried Canadian bacon or ham and fresh-baked biscuits.

Two simple ingredients—mango juice and sugar—
cook to create a sweet sauce of honeylike
consistency. No bees required!

Mango Honey

5 medium mangoes (about
   4 lb.), seeded, peeled, and
   cut up (see page 127)

10 cups water

4 cups sugar

1. Place mangoes in a large pot. Cover with the water. Bring to boiling; reduce heat to low. Simmer, covered, about 20 minutes or until mangoes are very soft. Use a potato masher to lightly mash mangoes.

2. Line a colander with a double layer of 100-percent-cotton cheesecloth; place over a large bowl. Pour crushed mangoes into colander. Let stand for 30 minutes, pressing gently occasionally to extract the juice. Measure 8 cups juice.

3. In the same pot stir together the juice and sugar. Bring to boiling. Boil, uncovered, at a moderate, steady rate about 2 hours or until the mixture is slightly thickened (the consistency of warm honey) and reduced to 4 cups, stirring occasionally to prevent sticking. Quickly skim off foam with a metal spoon.

4. Ladle hot mixture into hot, sterilized half-pint canning jars, leaving a ¼-inch headspace. Wipe jar rims; adjust lids and screw bands.

5. Process filled jars in a boiling-water canner 10 minutes (start timing when water returns to boiling). Remove jars from canner; cool on wire racks. **Makes 4 half-pint jars.**

PER 1 TABLESPOON: 58 cal., 0 g fat, 0 mg chol., 0 mg sodium, 15 g carb., 15 g sugars, 0 g fiber, 0 g pro.

Sweet Gifts

Good Morning!

Brighten your breakfast or brunch table with these rise-and-shine designs.

Create sun and cloud shapes from scrapbooking paper. Use a white pencil to write on the cloud. Affix shapes to jar using crafts glue.

You are my SUNSHINE

Invert a decorative paper cupcake liner over the top of the lid. Tie with colored twine. Give with a small decorative spreader, if desired.

Create a citrus slice and leaves from scrapbooking paper. Line lid with a coordinating paper circle; secure with screw band. Punch holes in citrus slice and leaves, and attach to jar rim using ribbon.

Tart Cherry-Coffee Preserves

Cut a circle of newspaper and place on top of the lid. Screw the screw band back onto the jar. Cut an edge of washi tape with scallop scissors; adhere to rim of screw band. Add a sticker label.

Fresh Picked

These blooms don't need water. Present a floral gift that is sweet enough for the honey bees.

Cut a stem and leaves from green tape; affix to side of jar. Use leaves to label jar. Cut a circle from scrapbooking paper; place on top of lid. Cut petals from paper. Affix petals to neck of jar using crafts glue. Screw the screw band back onto the jar.

Honey dew Jelly

Lemon-Lime

Line lid with scrapbooking paper circle; secure with screw band. Tape colored tissue festooning to rim of screw band.

Cut a square from a floral handkerchief or paper napkin and place on top of the lid. Screw the screw band back onto the jar.

Line lid with scrapbooking paper; secure with screw band. Cut an edge of decorative tape with scallop scissors; adhere to rim of screw band. Tie a colored label on jar with colored baker's twine. Decorate with stickers.

Apricot-Rosemary Jelly

Holiday Cheer

Spread some holiday happiness throughout the year with seasonally adorned jars.

Tie jar with wide plaid ribbon. Create label using a small wooden deer. Affix label and tree cupcake topper to top of jar with hot glue.

Balsamic-Basil Plum Jam

Line lid with glittered scrapbooking paper circle; secure with screw band. Adhere decorative tape to rim of screw band. Cut hearts from same paper. Tie colorful baker's twine around rim; affix hearts to twine using crafts glue. Add X and O letter stickers.

Place a Halloween-patterned cocktail napkin on top of the jar. Secure with black ribbon. Affix toy spider to jar using crafts glue.

Peach & Sriracha Pepper Jam

Tie single-strand floral garland around jar. Add a colorful sticker label.

Cut a circle of colorful tissue paper and place on top of the lid. Screw the screw band back onto the jar. Wrap rim of screw band with green masking tape. Tie ribbon around rim; add bells to ends.

Vintage Chic

Retro is trendy (just like canning!) when you dress up your jars with bold patterned oilcloth.

Cut strips of oilcloth in a mix of widths and adhere to the top and bottom of the jar using double-stick tape. Screw on the screw band to hold in place.

Cut squares of chalkboard oilcloth and patterned oilcloth. Tie to the jar using twine.

Cut one wide strip of oilcloth and wrap around the jar. Adhere to the jar using double-stick tape.

Cut a square of oilcloth and place on top of the lid. Screw the screw band back onto the jar.

Cut a square of oilcloth. Place the jar in the center of the square and pull the corners of the cloth up around the jar. Tie with twine.

JAM

Troubleshooting

Here's a rundown of some common jam-making problems and their solutions.

PROBLEM	CAUSE	SOLUTION
Contains crystals	The amount of sugar or cooking time may have been off or the method was wrong.	Measure sugar and other ingredients precisely. Cook traditional jams for the specified time. Cooking too little doesn't allow sugar to dissolve; cooking too long results in excess evaporation. If sugar crystals stick to side of pan during cooking, carefully wipe them off before filling jars.
Too soft or runny	Pectin, which interacts with natural and added sugars and acid, didn't develop properly.	Measure sugar, pectin, and other ingredients precisely. Do not double recipes for jams and jellies. Jams have not boiled long enough at a rolling boil. Do not shake or turn jars while cooling; this breaks pectin bonds.
Contains bubbles	Spoilage or trapped air.	If bubbles are moving when the jar is still, the preserves have spoiled and should be discarded. If the bubbles are not moving when the jar is still, the jam was not ladled quickly enough into the jar. Also, pour the jam to the side of the jar rather than directly into the center of the jar to prevent bubbles.
Mold occurs during storage	Too much headspace or improper processing.	Make sure to leave a ¼-inch headspace with jams and jellies. Measure carefully. Process for the time specified in a current, reliable recipe. Never use a wax seal. This outdated method encourages spoilage.
Too stiff or tough	Overcooking; too much sugar; or too much natural pectin in fruit.	Make sure to use fruit that is fully ripe, not underripe. Make sure not to exceed 220°F when cooking. If not adding pectin, use ¾ cup sugar to 1 cup juice.
Color seems dark	Overcooking or stored improperly.	Avoid long boiling; do not exceed 220°F. Store jars in a cool, dry, dark place and use within 1 year. Refrigerate after opening.

Altitude Adjustments

Water boils at a lower temperature at higher altitudes, which means that when canning at higher elevations, you must process food longer in a boiling-water canner. Check your altitude online at veloroutes.org/elevation before you begin canning and adjust processing times as shown in the chart below.

FEET ABOVE SEA LEVEL	INCREASE IN PROCESSING TIME
1,001 to 3,000	5 minutes
3,001 to 6,000	10 minutes
Above 6,000	15 minutes

Index

Metric Information

PRODUCT DIFFERENCES

Most of the ingredients called for in the recipes in this book are available in most countries. However, some are known by different names. Here are some common American ingredients and their possible counterparts:

- Sugar (white) is granulated, fine granulated, or castor sugar.
- Powdered sugar is icing sugar.
- All-purpose flour is enriched bleached or unbleached white household flour. When self-rising flour is used in place of all-purpose flour in a recipe that calls for leavening, omit the leavening agent (baking soda or baking powder) and salt.
- Light-color corn syrup is golden syrup.
- Cornstarch is cornflour.
- Baking soda is bicarbonate of soda.
- Vanilla or vanilla extract is vanilla essence.
- Green, red, or yellow sweet peppers are capsicums or bell peppers.
- Golden raisins are sultanas.

VOLUME AND WEIGHT

The United States traditionally uses cup measures for liquid and solid ingredients. The chart (above right) shows the approximate imperial and metric equivalents. If you are accustomed to weighing solid ingredients, the following approximate equivalents will be helpful.

- 1 cup butter, castor sugar, or rice = 8 ounces = ½ pound = 250 grams
- 1 cup flour = 4 ounces = ¼ pound = 125 grams
- 1 cup icing sugar = 5 ounces = 150 grams
- Canadian and U.S. volume for a cup measure is 8 fluid ounces (237 ml), but the standard metric equivalent is 250 ml.
- 1 British imperial cup is 10 fluid ounces.
- In Australia, 1 tablespoon equals 20 ml, and there are 4 teaspoons in the Australian tablespoon.
- Spoon measures are used for small amounts of ingredients. Although the size of the tablespoon varies slightly in different countries, for practical purposes and for recipes in this book, a straight substitution is all that's necessary. Measurements made using cups or spoons always should be level unless stated otherwise.

COMMON WEIGHT RANGE REPLACEMENTS

Imperial / U.S.	Metric
½ ounce	15 g
1 ounce	25 g or 30 g
4 ounces (¼ pound)	115 g or 125 g
8 ounces (½ pound)	225 g or 250 g
16 ounces (1 pound)	450 g or 500 g
1¼ pounds	625 g
1½ pounds	750 g
2 pounds or 2¼ pounds	1,000 g or 1 Kg

OVEN TEMPERATURE EQUIVALENTS

Fahrenheit Setting	Celsius Setting	Gas Setting
300°F	150°C	Gas Mark 2 (very low)
325°F	160°C	Gas Mark 3 (low)
350°F	180°C	Gas Mark 4 (moderate)
375°F	190°C	Gas Mark 5 (moderate)
400°F	200°C	Gas Mark 6 (hot)
425°F	220°C	Gas Mark 7 (hot)
450°F	230°C	Gas Mark 8 (very hot)
475°F	240°C	Gas Mark 9 (very hot)
500°F	260°C	Gas Mark 10 (extremely hot)
Broil	Broil	Grill

*Electric and gas ovens may be calibrated using celsius. However, for an electric oven, increase celsius setting 10 to 20 degrees when cooking above 160°C. For convection or forced air ovens (gas or electric), lower the temperature setting 25°F/10°C when cooking at all heat levels.

BAKING PAN SIZES

Imperial / U.S.	Metric
9×1½-inch round cake pan	22- or 23×4-cm (1.5 L)
9×1½-inch pie plate	22- or 23×4-cm (1 L)
8×8×2-inch square cake pan	20×5-cm (2 L)
9×9×2-inch square cake pan	22- or 23×4.5-cm (2.5 L)
11×7×1½-inch baking pan	28×17×4-cm (2 L)
2-quart rectangular baking pan	30×19×4.5-cm (3 L)
13×9×2-inch baking pan	34×22×4.5-cm (3.5 L)
15×10×1-inch jelly roll pan	40×25×2-cm
9×5×3-inch loaf pan	23×13×8-cm (2 L)
2-quart casserole	2 L

U.S. / STANDARD METRIC EQUIVALENTS

⅛ teaspoon = 0.5 ml	
¼ teaspoon = 1 ml	
½ teaspoon = 2 ml	
1 teaspoon = 5 ml	
1 tablespoon = 15 ml	
2 tablespoons = 25 ml	
¼ cup = 2 fluid ounces = 50 ml	
⅓ cup = 3 fluid ounces = 75 ml	
½ cup = 4 fluid ounces = 125 ml	
⅔ cup = 5 fluid ounces = 150 ml	
¾ cup = 6 fluid ounces = 175 ml	
1 cup = 8 fluid ounces = 250 ml	
2 cups = 1 pint = 500 ml	
1 quart = 1 litre	